The humor, history
and hallucinations of

Quinlan &
Jones

The philosopher and the jarhead.
Old cowboys and their
western ponderings.

Illustrations by John Bardwell

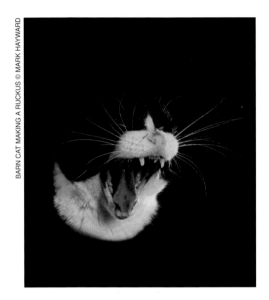

BARN CAT MAKING A RUCKUS © MARK HAYWARD

Vess Quinlan and Bill Jones, cowboys both (in one form or another), claim, "We ain't making this stuff up." Also known as the philosopher and the jarhead, these country boys couldn't qualify for entry into an Ivy League faculty lounge even in a waiter's outfit, which is no problem because deep-thinking pipe-smoking eggheads don't interest them. Neither do dead kings, forgotten wars and meaningless dates. But they do have some deep thoughts about the American West and real people and critters that make it interesting, odd and pretty funny. And this from two guys who never saw a faculty lounge.

Publisher/Editor: C.J. Hadley
Associate Editor: Alice Karpel
Designer/Illustrator: John Bardwell
Proofreader: Denyse Pellettiere White

Library of Congress Cataloging-in-Publication Data
Hadley, C.J.
Quinlan & Jones
ISBN #978-0-9647456-2-9
Library of Congress Control Number: 2020914690

Published by Range Conservation Foundation & RANGE magazine, Carson City, Nevada.

Hot Mail
Out on the range in Railroad Valley, Nevada.
© Larry Angier

The Philosopher & the Jarhead

Thinkin' western, thinkin' back.

Vess Quinlan spent most of his life raising livestock and growing alfalfa. For a while he ran national political campaigns, "but I learned quickly that 'truth' can be manipulated."

He was born a year and two weeks before Pearl Harbor was bombed and his dad and uncles enlisted to fight in World War II. For the next five years, his dog Corky, Tee Hee, Sheriff Murray Wilson and hobos living in a nearby camp were his best friends and mentors.

When he was eleven, Vess contracted polio and was hospitalized for close to a year. He was told to "lay still and do nothing," so he read a lot and learned a lot. By the time he hit fifteen, he was ready to do the things he was told were impossible for a crippled kid. After close to eighty years and one hell of a life, he proved the naysayers wrong.

Vess married Arla out of high school and they had "three good kids," eventually ranching and farming in the high cold country of southern Colorado. He tried a lot of things—some good, some bad—and several of those experiences are shared within.

Age took him out of full-time ranching so he now works as an occasional cowboy poet and writer, as a member of the board of the Western Folklife Center and a full-time long-haul trucker, because, he says, "I lack a retirement gene."

Bill Jones is living in exile from Wyoming and raises Angus-cross cattle in the hills of Tennessee. "I am still trying to figure out how to make money with eighty momma cows on a nonprofit farm."

A regular contributor to RANGE magazine, "because it's cheaper than psychotherapy and generates interesting mail," he claims that a memoir of his reluctant participation as a Marine in the Vietnam War, "Body Burning Detail," was not written to make money. "That aspect," he says, "has worked out splendidly."

In 2019, Vess and Bill were invited—all expenses paid—to share their poetry at the Library of Congress in conjunction with the Veterans History Project. Bill says he was previously opposed to taxpayer-funded artist events, "but now I have changed my mind."

Never known to control the keyboard, Bill sees no reason to change now. He continues to be irritated by low cattle prices, national politics, the TSA and anyone under sixty. Before moving to Wyoming to fulfill his cowboy fantasy, Bill was a uniformed officer and detective for close to twenty years. He has a bachelor's degree from the University of South Carolina and a master's in criminal justice from the University of Alabama.

Quinlan and Jones have unique and politically incorrect views of the world. They are a pair to draw to. You will like these country boys.—*CJH*

Peek a Moo
Five-year-old Waylon S. Dell'Orto at Elliott Joses' calf branding in San Andreas, California. © Robin Dell'Orto

Contents

"What are those boys thinking?"
The eagle watches. © Mark Hayward

The House of Hoover   8
Home to gentle things of great value.

Confessions of a Wannabe Cowboy   10
*I was so green I could hide out
on your lawn.*

A Shot Heard Around the Country   12
A skunk alarm causes chaos.

Life in the Mountains   14
It was sunny when I left this morning.

**Snakes, Cowboys, Religion
& Other Mysteries**   16
Watch out for lack of faith.

Bad Companions   18
Boys will be boys...sometimes.

Spoil the Rod, Save the Calf   20
A case of too much attention.

Buster & Billy Burro   24
Oh, no! Not child rearing!

The Cowboy Way   26
There's one more thing...

Riding the Cowboy Poetry Trail   28
Attempting to be "atmosphere."

A Boy Among Men   30
The lie of omission.

A Shepherd's Lament, Part I   36
*Quit bad-mouthing watermelon
and fried chicken.*

Lessons from Leo   38
*There was little evidence to support
my theory that I could run a ranch.*

Five More Miles   42
A serious disagreement.

**Cowboy Poetry, Oxymorons
& Baxter Black**   44
*Never one to let sleeping snakes lie, I continue
to dig myself into a matrimonial pit.*

It Behooves Me   47
Boots and shadows.

The Man of Many Uncles   48
I don't need a Ph.D. to water potatoes.

Double Duty   52
Skipping and hosing.

**Gambling, Rambling, Ranching
& Rehab**   54
Are six bred heifers a herd?

Pocket Gopher Stew   56
Tales from Stuttering Bill.

Confessions of a Capitalist Pig   60
Watch out for the tax man with his grubby little hand out.

Under the Big Sky   63
Mothering up.

New Boots for Bob   64
A gift from Santa.

The Bridge to No Where   66
Maybe that's "some where."

A Shepherd's Lament, Part II   68
Lowering standards at the Dew Drop Inn Café & Bar.

The Lost Bull   70
Closer than you think.

Ranching, Goat Yoga & Financial Freedom   72
If you think the Praying Cow Pose is difficult, try doing it with a goat standing on your back.

The Legend of Tom Munn   74
From classic to cowboy.

It's a Dog's Life   76
Rolling, waiting, flying.

Part Monkey
Larry Ponte loads cattle in the fall at Silver Lake, California. © Robin Dell'Orto

Good Dogs, Bad Dogs   78
Heretics and true believers.

Working Kids   82
Looping and checking.

Leo & Leatherwood's Wedding   84
A lack of fashion sense in upscale Texas.

Geezerhood Blues   86
If you have a degree in Elizabethan literature, it isn't my fault.

You Can't Make This Stuff Up   88
These guys are funny!

Of Mice and Women   90
Charles Darwin would be proud.

Fighting With a Gobbler   92
Learning about my past.

Ranching, Blasphemy & Other Unpardonable Sins   96
Without sin, politics, at least as we know it, would cease to exist.

Grandpas, Fathers & Sons   98
Simply tradition.

Busted!   100
Dammit, Bill, why did you let me see you?

Slouching Toward Geezerhood   102
To me, a Smart Phone is a Chinese puzzle.

The Ginger Belgians   104
Mr. McPherson's advice.

I've Got It!   107
Two-year-old cowgirl readies her rope.

Bilko   108
A schemer, scammer and talented con artist.

Hallelujah!   111
Cowgirls celebrate.

The House of Hoover

Home to gentle things of great value.

The old man was called Tee Hee. His roommate was a pack rat named Hoover. Maybe Hoover had heard the war stories late at night and might know what happened in World War I to cause Tee Hee to fear crowds, but none of the townfolk knew because the old veteran would not speak of it. The terrible stories would be safe with Hoover because he, like most pack rats, was secretive.

Why this talkative five-year-old and his live-wire border collie named Corky were the only living creatures except Hoover to be invited into the old fellow's clean but cluttered shack is a mystery. The shack itself was an architectural marvel constructed entirely of material salvaged from the town dump. I thought it wonderfully cozy and considered it much more interesting than our family home.

Tea, with a drop of Watkins lemon extract, was served in pale-blue china cups from a barely battered silver-plated teapot rescued from the dump. There was always a fresh soup bone for Corky. I would usually bring cookies from home for the old man and me to eat with our tea and a few peanuts for Hoover.

Tee Hee was allowed to live in the little shack beside the town dump, I suppose, because people with sons or brothers involved in the Second World War tended to tolerate the eccentricities of men from the First. When the older town kids surrounded and teased him, Tee Hee lost his ability to speak and could only shout "teeeee heeee" in a high-pitched wail and shake his walking stick. The kids

© JOHN BARDWELL

nicknamed him for the affliction and few knew his real name.

The town barber who cashed the old man's pension checks and kept his hair neatly trimmed knew. Everyone else called him Tee Hee. He even came to refer to himself as Tee Hee.

"Tomorrow," he would say, "Tee Hee's check will come and we will buy candy for the children."

His meager monthly check was enough to buy a few groceries, a

8

trinket for Hoover to hide, soup bones for Corky, and a sack of hard candy as a peace offering to the town kids.

I became candy master on pension check day, charged with distributing the sugary treats fairly to each clamoring child because Tee Hee could not allow anyone else near him. Corky served as sergeant at arms and maintained order. A growl and a few convincing snaps narrowly missing an aggressor made it clear that sudden moves toward the candy master were rude and would not be tolerated.

I always saved a brightly colored piece of hard candy for Hoover, who apparently thought it too pretty to eat and would promptly hide the prize in his wooden box. Tee Hee had converted a small box into a perfect pack-rat residence. He had even burned an address on the front of the hardwood box with a hot nail. Hoover lived at 12 Pack-Rat Boulevard. It was twelve because he came to live with Tee Hee on December 12, 1944.

The old man had carved a rat-sized hole for Hoover's private entrance and built a shelf just below the hole for an exercise balcony and observation post.

Corky and Hoover maintained an uneasy truce. He was a wise rat and knew that dogs, even one as well mannered as Corky, were not to be trusted. At first, Hoover would show only a twitching nose and beady black eyes at the hole with Corky or me in the shack, but eventually he accepted us and would come out on his balcony to groom himself and keep watch. The dog would lie quietly. He understood the pack rat was off-limits, but he followed the little creature's every move with his eyes. Hoover was right. Corky would have made short work of him had we not been there sipping lemon-extract-laced tea and keeping the peace.

The old man and I would prowl the dump in search of objects worth saving. Items deemed too good to throw away were collected and stacked neatly in Tee Hee's yard. Having personally seen the starvation and deprivation caused by war, Tee Hee would shake his head when he found still-usable things in good condition in the dump and mutter: "They don't understand. They just don't know."

When Corky got bored with the saving game, he would take off on his own excursions. Probably trying to find and assassinate one of Hoover's distant cousins in the kangaroo-rat clan, he would sometimes be late for tea-and-soup-bone time. One of those days, with Corky gone, Hoover climbed up to sit on the arm of the old man's chair and groom himself. I reached out to pet him. The little fellow squeaked in fear and ran to his box.

Tee Hee patiently explained that Hoover was not a pet. "Hoover," he said, "is not like Corky. He is his own rat and a free creature. Never try to touch him or pick him up like you would a kitten. Hoover might bite off your finger. He has chosen to live here but could get along nicely without our help."

Tee Hee died in his sleep one bitter night in January, a few months after my dad and uncles came home from World War II. Sheriff Murray Wilson found an amazing collection of the old soldier's combat medals packed carefully in a large Prince Albert tobacco can.

My old friend was given a funeral with full military honors and buried in a tiny cemetery not a hundred yards from his little shack. I still have a shell casing Dad brought me from the salute fired in Tee Hee's honor.

The old veteran left his mark and taught a lonely little boy many gentle things of great value. The best were how to make do with what others throw away and how to respect and befriend dignified creatures like Hoover.

I like to think that Hoover lived out his days comfortably at 12 Pack-Rat Boulevard.—*VQ*

Confessions of a Wannabe Cowboy

I was so green I could hide out in your lawn.

To be a cowboy I guess it might help to know a little something about cows. At the very least, a guy should be able to tell the difference between a steer and a heifer—that is a good place to start anyway. I did not know straight up about cows when I first moved to Wyoming, the Cowboy State, so I took a ranch management course at the local community college. Instead of growing broke slowly, it teaches you how to go belly up financially in eighteen months or less.

Although I learned a lot about ranch economics—it is far better to have more money coming in than going out—I was still having a little trouble distinguishing between bulls, steers, heifers, old and young cows, and how to make money raising livestock. I knew drastic action was in order. (Now after thirty-some years I have become reasonably skilled at determining bovine sexual characteristics, but I still can't figure out the money part....)

I met a local rancher, Rick, at church one Sunday and soon call him up. I ask if I can come out to his place and learn about the cow business. There is a long silence on his end of the phone.

"You don't expect to get paid, do you?" he finally asks. I assure him this is strictly an educational exercise. He reluctantly agrees. Back then I don't even have a horse, saddle or any other basic cowboy stuff a guy needs, wants or just must have because he saw Clint Eastwood (Rowdy) with one just like it on "Rawhide." For several years I go out to the ranch and help gather, brand, ship, doctor or whatever. Once Rick and I spend several days riding a 100,000-acre BLM allotment searching for some cows before he remembers he sold those cows the previous year. I wrote a pretty good cowboy poem about it.

It takes Rick about a year to warm up. We are good friends now, but he told me he initially thought I had some ulterior motives and he also had a sneaking suspicion I was going to try to recruit him as an Amway distributor. I don't know how much help I ever was. Mostly I just asked a lot of dumb questions. I was so green I could hide out in your lawn. Also, I started riding horses late in life; therefore, all I ever did to improve my horseback skills merely raised my level of mediocrity. Later, me and my horse, Poco, became extremely adept at blocking gates and riding back to the ranch for a couple of beers.

In that first year Rick calls and says we are going to "preg check" some cows on Saturday. I have no idea what that means and am ashamed to ask. I figure the local veterinarian will come out, take some blood tests, ship the sample to Cheyenne, and if the rabbit dies, you will receive a notice in the mail that Cow Number 565 is now in a "family way."

That isn't what happens. Doc Perkins comes out with a rubber glove up to his shoulder and a snorkel. He needs both. For the first few cows going through the chute I think this may be someone's idea of a sick practical joke. After 350 cows I realize they are serious. The next week we fertility test a bunch of herd bulls. I am not even going to begin to explain *that* process, so don't worry.

Doc Perkins comes out with a rubber glove up to his shoulder and a snorkel. He needs both. For the first few cows going through the chute I think this may be someone's idea of a sick practical joke.

Anyway, one day Rick calls up and asks if I can come out to the ranch the next day and help move some cows. "Bring Poco," he adds. This is really the first time he has ever called me directly. I am thinking I must be making a pretty good hand. Maybe he needs another gate blocked and Poco and me will be on it like snow on the Rockies. (Much later, Rick confesses he had already called everyone he knew in two counties and I was the only person available.)

Anyway, it is a great day at the ranch. We move cows from the lower pasture down by the river up to a newer pasture near the ranch house. Rick only loses his temper four times and there are only two minor disasters. We narrowly avoid at least one semi-catastrophe. In other words, a normal ranch day.

At day's end, over a couple of cold ones, Rick pays me one of the nicest compliments I ever got in my time as a wannabe Wyoming cowboy. It was especially touching because Rick always says what he means and means what he says and does not give praise lightly.

"Today," Rick pronounces solemnly, "you didn't get in the way all that much...."

I got misty eyed and had to look away.—*BJ*

California Cowboy
Mattley Dell'Orto branding calves in Plymouth, California.
When everyone was asked to wear a goofy shirt, he succeeded.
© Robin Dell'Orto

A Shot Heard Around the Country

A skunk alarm causes chaos.

Grandma intended to keep the chickens laying eggs all winter and that meant a lot of work building a snug chicken house with six inches of dirt packed between double walls. When we had finally hauled enough wheelbarrow loads of dirt to fill and pack the five-feet-high walls, Grandpa and my uncles helped place the heavy vegas (log rafters) on top of the sturdy walls. The vegas had to be strong enough to support the insulating dirt that was poured on top of the lumber-and-tarpaper roof.

I built impressive muscles for a ten-year-old boy by serving as Grandma's chief laborer. When our masterpiece was finished, Grandpa and my uncles stooped over and entered to inspect our work and praise our accomplishment.

The chicken hostel was built to Grandma's dimensions. She was barely five feet tall when standing on a brick. Grandpa and my uncles stood well over six feet. The chickens fit nicely.

The trouble came when an old cowboy friend of Grandpa's stopped to say goodbye. A nephew had pulled some strings and got the old man a room in the Old Cowboy's Home in Bandera, Texas.

The chicken hostel was built to Grandma's dimensions. She was barely five feet tall when standing on a brick. Grandpa and my uncles stood well over six feet. The chickens fit nicely.

He would be leaving Colorado the next day.

"I want you to have this," the old cowboy said to Grandpa, and carefully lifted out of a nest of blankets in the pickup bed the biggest rifle I had ever seen.

"Well, I'll be damned! A Sharps .45-90 buffalo gun. I did not know there were any still around."

"I don't expect they'll let me keep it at the home and I know you'll take good care of it. This old rifle might be worth something someday."

Uncle Buster was fifteen that year and wanted to fire the gun right away but Grandpa said the old piece might blow up in Buster's face and he should put it in the gun cabinet with the other rifles. The box of huge shells was placed on the shelf with the other boxes of ammunition.

About two o'clock one morning, the chickens sent up a skunk alarm. Grandpa grabbed a flashlight and hollered at Buster to get the gun. Buster, not one to squander a golden opportunity, dragged the old buffalo gun out of the gun closet and loaded it.

© JOHN BARDWELL

Grandpa was standing in his boots and long johns all hunched over with the light on the skunk. The skunk was cowering in the corner. The chickens were witnesses.

Buster laid the barrel of the heavy rifle on one of the roosts, pointed it at the skunk and pulled the trigger. It sounded like a bomb had gone off in the chicken house, startling Grandma and me standing on the back porch a hundred feet away.

I don't remember if Grandma was rubbing Watkins Pain Oil on four or five knots on Grandpa's head. The vegas were undamaged. Buster had a large bruise from the recoil. The skunk was vaporized. The chickens were shell-shocked and didn't lay another egg all winter. If he had dared to say a word, Buster might have argued that Grandpa had not said exactly which rifle to bring to the skunk killing.

Several things happened as a result of this incident. We had to buy eggs from a neighboring ranch. Grandpa spent a lot of time wondering why he ever had kids in the first place. Buster came off best since he got to brag about being the only kid in the county to actually kill a skunk, at close quarters, with a buffalo gun.—*VQ*

Life in the Mountains

Coping with harsh weather extremes is part of everyday ranching in the mountain West. It was sunny and sixty degrees that morning when the cowboys left the Darwin Ranch, an inholding in the Bridger-Teton National Forest outside Pinedale, Wyoming. © Skip Klein

Snakes, Cowboys, Religion & Other Mysteries

Watch out for lack of faith.

Snakes have never been my favorite animals. Especially poisonous ones. I like frogs (especially after you fry their tiny legs in beer batter), but snakes—since that little strange episode with the talking snake in the Garden of Eden—never have been very popular.

In the Appalachian region of the United States, where I am currently in exile from Wyoming, there is a religious sect that likes to handle poisonous snakes as part of their religious service. It seems there is a verse in the Bible that says believers can "take up serpents and not be harmed." So that is exactly what they do during church services. They pass around rattlesnakes, copperheads, water moccasins, and even cobras.

I ain't, by the way, making this up. I even know some of these folks—at least some of the ones still breathing and walking among us. It is more common than you may think. And *nobody* goes to sleep during these services, I can assure you. In fact, there has never been a reported incident of anyone even yawning. This has been going on for a hundred years or so. So far, over two hundred people have died from snakebite. Thousands more have been bitten—many several

Olin, the snake handler. At two years old, he shot and killed this snake at the 7V Ranch in Alpine, Texas. He did not use it in a religious ceremony.

hundred times. After being bitten, they do not seek medical treatment as that obviously would show a "lack of faith." (I would show a humongous lack of faith in that I would not pick up one of the wiggly little boogers in the first place.)

God has never told me to pick up a poisonous snake. Or any snake, for that matter. Even if He did, I think I would have to argue a little. The Old Testament is full of folks arguing with God. Jonah, who was swallowed by a "big fish," comes immediately to mind. Now that I think about it, neither option—picking up a copperhead or being unceremoniously gulped by a fish—seems that appealing.

One snake handling preacher I know is in prison now on a matter unrelated to his snake handling proclivities. It is my fervent hope that perhaps he can start a snake handling ministry within the prison walls—maybe in the cop killer and child molester wing. Another snake handling believer I know is named after a famous rock-and-roll singer. In the interest of respecting his privacy I will not reveal his name, other than to say his first name rhymes with "pelvis." It has been a few years since I heard much about him. Perhaps he has decided to go to a snake-free and more traditional house of worship. The other possibility is that while handling snakes...well, we won't go there.

An interesting footnote to these snake handling churches is that some members, dissatisfied with just draping rattlesnakes around their necks, have taken to drinking poison during church services. Another form of "faith testing." This works about like you would expect. Strychnine, a deadly poison, has unfortunately whittled down the membership of many of these churches. At least one church member I read about, displeased with merely surviving the snakes and poison, decides to stick his finger in a wall socket. He survives, but it is a *shocking* incident nonetheless. (Sorry for the bad pun. I can't help myself.)

I do know a couple of guys who have been bitten by poisonous snakes, but they were not in church at the time. Both were working in their vegetable gardens. Paul, my one friend, says the bite felt like someone smashed him in the ankle with a sledgehammer. He saw a copperhead make a fast getaway and immediately called his sister, a nurse who lives down the road, for medical advice. She told him to get his butt to the hospital posthaste. Good advice. The other guy was reaching for a cucumber and a six-foot-long rattler sank its fangs into the fleshy part of his thumb. Both men spent several days in ICU and survived. Both agree it was an extremely unpleasant experience.

Anyway, a few years ago a *New York Times* reporter is sent down South to write an article about this bizarre snake handling phenomenon. He becomes friends with some snake handling preachers, starts attending churches, and, alas, before you know it he begins "taking up serpents" himself.

"I guess you might say I got caught up in it," says Dennis

Nobody goes to sleep during these services. In fact, there has never been a reported incident of anyone even yawning.

Covington. A professional journalist and family man, he finally drops out of the snake handling scene when he realizes, "I was in over my head." (No kidding!) He details the entire experience in his book, "Salvation on Sand Mountain." It is a page turner and—unlike a six-foot timber rattler—you will not want to put it down.

At least some of the folks written about in the book are no longer with us. The Reverend "Punkin" Brown, a semi-famous snake handling preacher, dies an agonizing death after being snakebit in a church service. True to his faith, he refuses any medical assistance. His wife takes over his church and sometime later she meets the same unfortunate end. Jamie Coots, who pastored a church not far from where I now live, succumbed to a poisonous snakebite just a couple of years ago. Despite my best creative efforts, I am unable to write anything witty, humorous or profound about any of these tragic, meaningless deaths. A number of children are left to carry on the best they can.

I did hear a pretty good tale about a Wyoming cowboy who inadvertently attended one of the snake handling church meetings. In search of some spiritual sustenance, no one informed him this wasn't a regular church service. Our cowboy, by the way, was not partial to snakes at all—dead or alive. And he had no idea the minister was going to bring out a whole box of poisonous, slithering snakes. It was a big surprise. Not only that, but the snakes were between him and the front door.

So he asks the woman sitting in the pew next to him where the back door is, in order that he might make a timely and quick exit.

"Well," she says, "they ain't got no back door here."

"Where then," our cowboy asks, "do you think they would like one?"—*BJ*

Bad Companions

Boys will be boys...sometimes.

I had to spank him today," I heard Mom tell Dad just before I went to sleep.

"What for?"

"Hiding from the sheriff."

"I bet that didn't work. Murray Wilson has been a lawman for thirty years. He knows how to find bad guys. A five-year-old desperado and his dog won't scare Murray."

"It's not funny. I don't worry when he runs away to visit Tee Hee in his little shack by the dump. The old man might be shell-shocked and strange but wouldn't hurt anybody. It scares me when he goes to the hobo jungle by the river. There are strange men coming and going from that camp all the time. Who knows what kind of men are there? I hear some of them are even communist organizers for the Industrial Workers of the World."

"Where did Murray find him this time?"

"With the hobos. Murray told me one of them was playing throw the stick with Corky and your son was sitting on a log eating a bowl of greasy stew. They give him coffee! Little boys aren't supposed to drink coffee. Next thing he'll be smoking cigars and telling dirty stories. When he saw Murray coming, he ran and hid behind a pile of railroad ties. Corky thought they were playing hide and seek and helped Murray find him."

"Ah, betrayed by his best friend. How do you like that?"

"I told you! This is not funny."

"What do you want to do with him? Spanking doesn't work. Besides, Corky doesn't like the spanking business. You are going to get bit one of these days."

"You're not much help. Maybe I'll send him to work with you every day. At least he'd learn to run a bulldozer instead of how to be a good communist. Mrs. Luby told Mrs. Wilson she is afraid our son is a bad influence on her little Paul. It is embarrassing."

Paul was the only kid my age in the neighborhood. He lived with his lawyer father and mother in a big two-story house a few blocks east. I was occasionally allowed to visit and play in their yard. Paul, however, was never allowed to play in my yard. His mother did not like her son wandering off to visit strange old men who lived in shacks and she disapproved of hobnobbing with hobos.

One Friday afternoon, Corky and I were allowed to play in Paul's yard. His mother wore fancy dresses and smelled like a lilac bush. She looked at me suspiciously and said, "Don't you boys leave the yard. I am going to lie down. I have a bit of a headache."

It was probably all that lilac stuff.

I showed Paul the slingshot my cousin, Mick, had made. Mick was Eagle County's head mechanic and could make anything. He used a forked stick, red rubber from an inner tube, and a leather rock pocket made from an old boot top. The stretchy red rubber would send a rock like a bullet.

After I let him try and kill a sparrow with my new weapon, Paul said, "Boy, wish I had one."

"Mick could make you one. There are lots of good forked sticks in those willows behind the county shop. We could be back before

> **Paul was never allowed to play in my yard. His mother did not like her son wandering off to visit strange old men who lived in shacks and she disapproved of hobnobbing with hobos.**

your mother wakes up."

Paul looked dubious. We sneaked quietly into the house to check on his mother. She lay on her back snoring loudly. Her mouth was open expelling lilac fumes. We took off.

Mick made Paul a slingshot and set us up a row of cans behind the shop to practice shooting. One of us, probably Paul as he tended toward evil, noticed the row of little windows high up to let light into the shop. What happened next is predictable. What happened after that is also predictable.

Mick, hearing rocks hitting the tin building, decided he was under attack and called Murray Wilson.

Murray and his deputy screeched their 1936 Ford V8 cop cars to a stop blocking both ends of the alley. Murray leaned across the hood and shouted through a bullhorn. "Throw down your weapons and put your hands on top of your heads."

We complied. What happened next would cause lawsuits to fly like confetti these days. Murray handcuffed Paul and me and loaded us in the backseat. Paul was scared. I was used to it. Murray always brought me home in handcuffs. It was his little joke. Corky, the traitor, rode in the front seat. He loved Murray Wilson.

I expected Murray to take me home like he always did. Boy, was I wrong. Murray headed downtown at about two miles an hour. The deputy followed closely in case we tried to escape. Murray keyed his radio. "Better tell Margie [Murray's wife and cook for the jail] to lay in a big supply of salami. We got a couple of bad ones here. They will probably be in jail a long time. The old judge is fed up with hoodlums attacking county employees and trying to destroy county property."

I hated salami. Paul leaned over and whispered: "My dad is a lawyer and can get us out of jail. He does it all the time."

The whisper must have been too loud because Murray keyed his radio again and said: "I'll bet this Luby kid thinks he will get off easy 'cause his dad's a lawyer. He'll sure be surprised. The judge is still mad as hell over the sneaky lawyer trick the kid's dad pulled in the last trial. I'll bet he decides to make an example of these two."

Paul started to cry. I was wondering if I had finally gone too far. Murray locked us in the same cell. I think he slammed the door extra hard just for effect. It worked. Corky laid down beside Murray's desk and went to sleep.

Paul started crying again and tried to turn state's evidence. "It was his idea," he screamed, shaking the bars. "His cousin Mick made the slingshots. I wasn't supposed to leave the yard. He made me."

I never cared much for Paul after that.

Murray told Paul to shut up and said: "According to the law, you were an accomplice before, after, during, and throughout the fact. You, Paul Luby, are guilty as he is."

I suppose Murray sent the deputy right away to tell our mothers where we were, but it was way after dark before my dad showed up to take us home.

It is like Paul's mother feared and Murray said as we were leaving, "Bad companions will do you in every time."—*VQ*

Vess with cousin Bonney and with Corky, his favorite bad companion. Vess admits, "They were both troublemakers."

Spoil the Rod, Save the Calf

A case of too much attention.

A few years ago my buckaroo pal Rod McQueary was showing me around his Ruby Valley Ranch in Nevada. Actually, it was almost thirty years ago. Time, as they say, sure flies when you are having fun. It also flies by when you are not having any fun at all...as in the process of giving me the complete genetic and family history of each of his first-calf heifers. "Boring" is the key word here. This is the inevitable result of living on an isolated ranch so far out in the sticks that there is no decent television reception. Now that there is a satellite dish attached to the side of every ranch house in America, interest in animal genealogy takes a backseat to watching reruns of "Naked and Afraid."

The neighbor's bull jumped the fence and got into my replacement heifers," Rod complains. "The SOB was one of them big exotic bulls the size of a double-decker Greyhound bus. He throws a calf so big these heifers just can't push the boogers out."

Rod, ever the sagebrush philosopher, contemplates this for a minute. From past experience, I know a "pearl of wisdom" is in the formative stages of regurgitation. It comes soon enough. "When it comes to love and/or lust," Rod muses, "whether it be people or livestock, a barbed-wire fence just ain't much of a barrier."

Having had some experiences with love, lust, livestock and barbed wire—in various combinations—I nod vigorously in total agreement.

Rod then proceeds to cuss the neighbor's bull and fencing (or lack thereof), the county agent who suggested the neighbor get the bull in the first place, Secretary of the Interior Bruce Babbitt's mother for giving him birth, the country of origin of the bull (neither of us were exactly sure of the country so Rod settled on cussing the entire European continent), the high cost of fuel and fertilizer, various government agencies including the U.S. Postal Service, government employees in general and especially the county snowplow driver, the saddle horse that bucked him off three weeks ago, as well as other highly relevant subjects which due to the ravages of age and time have graciously faded from my memory.

Driving the pickup around the pasture we roll up behind a heifer lying down in obvious trouble. A big calf is halfway

"When it comes to love and/or lust, whether it be people or livestock, a barbed-wire fence just ain't much of a barrier."

out...stuck. Did you ever notice how every major wreck starts with what seems to be a good idea at the time? "The best laid plans of mice and men" often...well, you know the rest. Rod pauses from his rant (which is a good thing because he was running out of things and folks to cuss) and proceeds to light up like a Japanese pinball machine.

"I'll sneak up behind her and sit on her head so she can't get up," he instructs proudly. "You see if you can then pull the calf out."

"The neighbor's bull jumped the fence and got into my replacement heifers. The SOB was one of them big exotic bulls the size of a double-decker Greyhound bus. He throws a calf so big these heifers just can't push the boogers out."

Rod takes off before I can object and is tiptoeing up to the heifer like an errant husband sneaking back into the house after a night on the town. A few feet away he does a respectable swan dive and belly flops across the heifer's neck. She is not amused and quickly scrambles to her feet, convinced a space alien has dropped from the sky with evil intentions. She then tosses Rod at least thirty feet into the air. Being somewhat slow of foot, I am still in the pickup and get an excellent view of the whole event. While Rod is still airborne, I write the first two lines of what could be a classic cowboy poem. This is better than any television show. (Even "Naked and Afraid"? Well, maybe not so much.)

Rod's arms and legs are twirling like two windmills in a tropical hurricane. It occurs to me that if he could stay up just a little longer he may even learn to fly. But gravity eventually prevails and he rather unceremoniously

Rod McQueary, a great cowboy, soldier and poet, did everything with gusto. Both former Marines and Vietnam vets, Rod and Bill wrote a book of war poems together, "Blood Trails," in 1993. © Peter de Lory, Western Folklife Center

Bill Jones, above, met Rod McQueary at the National Cowboy Poetry Gathering in Elko, Nevada, in 1988. Bill maintains that this story is the truth, the whole truth and nothing but the truth. However, on the advice of his attorney, he will refuse any suggestion that he takes a polygraph. Rod passed away in December 2012.

returns to terra firma. Luckily for Rod a big rock breaks his fall.

By the time I get to Rod he is acting a little goofy. Or maybe "goofier" would be a better adjective here. Rod wants to know which way the ninjas went and is there any banana pudding left. The heifer? She takes off bellowing like a tugboat foghorn. The calf is swinging from her rear end like a grandfather clock pendulum gone berserk. She sure can run fast for an animal that was half dead a couple of minutes ago.

"Let's catch her!" Rod yells in what may be his second bad idea of the day. Rod assigns me to drive while he builds a loop while standing in the bed of the pickup. Bouncing along the pasture in pursuit, I catch a glimpse of Rod in the side-view mirror grinning like a mule eating briars. Another irrefutable sign of an entertainment-starved existence on a ranch fifty miles from town. Or could it could be Rod's recent attempt at wingless flight has caused some permanent and irreversible brain damage?

Rod, a pretty fair roper, catches her on his first throw, letting out a victory whoop like he has just won All-Around Cowboy at the National Finals Rodeo. We then snub the severely traumatized heifer to some willows by the creek, attach another rope to the calf, and use the pickup to ease the big bull calf out—none the worse for wear. Turning the heifer loose, she takes off for the neighbor's fence, perhaps in search of some sympathy from her foreign boyfriend. She wants nothing to do with us or her calf. Can't say I blame her.

Rod tells me later he never could find the heifer. (I am not sure he even looked.) But he did take the calf to the sale barn the next week. Said it weighed around 600 pounds.

We take the rest of the afternoon off. Back at the ranch house, much to our mutual dismay, it is discovered that someone has already eaten all the banana pudding.—*BJ*

That heifer took off for the neighbor's fence, perhaps in search of some sympathy from her foreign boyfriend. She wants nothing to do with us or her calf. Can't say I blame her. This Scottish Highland bull wasn't even on the same continent, but that girl had dreams!
© Alasdair Gillies, head stockman at Invercauld, Braemar, Scotland

Buster & Billy Burro

Oh, no! Not child rearing!

Vaudevillian W.C. Fields, although he famously hated children and animal acts, would likely feel sympathy for today's poor little tykes plagued as they are by goofy anticompetition policies where even the dumbest kid gets passing grades in high school, student loans for college, and where every clumsy all-thumbs clod gets a trophy in the tiddlywinks tournament. His greatest sympathy, however, would probably be reserved for the poor little devils hovered over by "helicopter parents" spawned by the latest parenting fad.

Thinking about the changes in child-raising theory reminds me of the time our family went to visit Milton and Olivee Yarberry. Milton was running a ranch in great wild country a few miles east of Wagon Mound, New Mexico. It must have been late fall 1949, because my little brother Van was four years old and sister Barbara was two. The ages of the three little Yarberrys matched ours but they were all boys.

Our parents were also about the same ages. Mom went to high school with Milton and Olivee was a distant cousin. Dad and Milton had both returned a few years before from serving in the South Pacific during World War II. Buster and I had apparently been conceived before the war. We were nine.

The ranch house was small but comfortable. All six children were banished to the living room so parents could enjoy a quiet visit over cards in the dining room. After the third time Milton had to come into the living room and order us to settle down and be quiet, he suggested Buster catch Billy and give us all a ride.

Most people do not think horses, mules, and burros have facial expressions, but when Billy Burro saw six rowdy children headed his way, the expression on his face and other body language clearly said, *"Oh, No!"*

Billy began racing around the small corral at top speed, apparently hoping a hole in the fence would magically appear so he could escape into the miles of canyons, hills, and grass that lay just outside. When none did, Billy stuck his head in a corner, apparently hoping we would just go away or be eaten by bears.

Buster got a rope out of the tack room and handed me a slim pole about six feet long and said: "Poke that stupid burro with this pole until he comes out of the corner and I will rope him as he runs by. Don't get too close or he will kick the hell out of you."

After I had administered several good pokes and deftly dodged a few well-aimed kicks, Billy spun out of the corner and ran by Buster. Billy was no fool and this was not his first rodeo. He managed to duck his head just as Buster threw the rope so it bounced off his withers. On the sixth try, Buster's timing was a hair better than Billy's and Billy was caught.

Milton had converted a horse-drawn manure spreader into a neat little two-wheeled cart. A pony harness, collar, and shiny brass-covered hames fit the little burro and an old work bridle complete with snaffle bit and blinders had been cut down to fit Billy perfectly.

When the rope settled around Billy's neck he became semicooperative and stood quietly while we harnessed him. He allowed the bridle to be slipped over his head. He would not, however, allow the snaffle bit to be placed in his mouth.

"Hold him a minute," Buster said, handing me the rope. He ran to the tack room and returned with a round stick whittled to a point. Buster shoved the stick between Billy's gums and pried his mouth open so I could insert the bit.

We hooked Billy to the cart, loaded the little kids in back, and Buster and I climbed up on the driver's seat and out the gate we went. There were no roads, just cow trails. Billy walked in the well-worn trail while the cart wheels bumped along through the grass.

One might think there were few trailside attractions to entertain tourists, but one would be wrong. Buster was a great tour guide. The first stop was a hole under a big rock in the side of a steep hill.

"That," Buster said, "is a rattlesnake den. It has been getting cold at night so they are in there rolled up in a big ball." Buster got down on his knees and stuck his head in the hole. "Come here," he said, "you can smell 'em."

We all took turns sticking our heads in the hole to smell the rattlesnakes. It was not a nice smell. Several minutes were spent discussing crawling in the hole and catching a snake to look at. Buster said the snakes would be asleep and they could not bite you when sleeping. My little brother volunteered to crawl in and get a snake, but the smell made him gag so we gave up on snake catching and spent an hour or so lying quietly beside prairie dog holes hoping one would come up so we could grab it. Buster said to catch them close to the head because they would bite you if they could.

Prairie dogs proved too clever to come up with predatory children breathing loudly near their holes.

There was a short-handled shovel in the cart so we decided to take turns digging on a badger hole we found. Our plan was to train the badger to do tricks, run away from home, and join the circus. We were sure a badger doing tricks would attract more people than a bearded lady or a two-headed calf.

It was a good thing we played out after an hour or two digging in the hard dirt and abandoned the badger plan. Badgers are cranky tough customers that would have made short work of a burro and six kids armed only with a rusty shovel.

We got back to the ranch just before dark, gave Billy an extra coffee can of oats and some fresh hay and headed for the house. The expression on all four parents' faces when six grimy, noisy, hungry kids burst into the room was exactly like that on Billy's face a few hours before. They were not exactly helicopter parents, but all six kids managed to survive the unenlightened parenting.—*VQ*

The Cowboy Way

Cowboy Office
"There's one more thing..." Whether branding cattle, doctoring a calf or fixing fence, Ian Tomlinson packs everything he might need in his truck. Ian owns the Vera Earl Ranches in Sonoita, Arizona, and he and his crew were branding calves when his cell phone rang. © Cheryl Rogos

Miniature Bull Fighter

"I've got work to do!"
Caseyn Pearson picks up the pieces at Jordan Valley's
Big Loop Rodeo in Oregon. © Carolyn Fox

Riding the Cowboy Poetry Trail

Attempting to be "atmosphere."

Baxter Black, esteemed cowboy poet, entertainer and bard to the agriculture masses, once remarked that cowboy poetry is "somewhere between 'good taste' and 'throwing up in your hat.'" How, may I ask, could anyone not like poetry with that kind of criteria? Personally, I got involved in the cowboy poetry deal kind of by accident. Like running out of gas. It is not anything you plan on, but is just one of those unfortunate things that happen. At one time I was wrangling dudes (Admittedly the lowest form of cowboyin'—in 1914 Gail Gardner's poem "The Dude Wrangler" ends with: "But when a feller turns dude wrangler, He ain't no good no more at all.") and I began reciting some of the old classic cowboy poems around the fire. Like the ill-fated dude wrangler in the poem, I couldn't quit it if I tried.

Later, I wrote some of my own poems—most of which were in the "throwin' up in your hat" class. Later, I got a little better and started getting invites here and there all around the country. (I was extremely popular at fertilizer conventions. I don't know why.)

© JOHN BARDWELL

Usually they paid for gas, a meal or two, and let me peddle the couple of books I cobbled together. Sometimes I broke even, other times I made a little money. I almost always had a good time.

One fall l get a phone call from a guy in Aspen, Colorado. Aspen, you may recall, is the place rich people believe they go when they die. He is the manager of a big exclusive hotel there. I won't tell you the name, but I suspect the owner is the same guy who invented those round little crackers served at parties. Figure it out. This next part is true—although I know some of you will think I am making this whole thing up. Well, I *ain't* making it up.

"Bill," the manager says, "we are having a little western-theme cocktail party next week and would like you to be with us."

"Should I do a few cowboy poems, a story or two?" I ask.

"No," he says, "that will not be necessary."

"Well," I counter, "I know four cowboy tunes with my guitar and two harmonica songs, would that be okay?"

"That will not be required either, Bill. Really, we are hosting a cocktail party for a bunch of New York stockbrokers and we want you to just stand around and be atmosphere."

I have never been "atmosphere" before, but it doesn't sound like it would be too hard. Nevertheless, I just don't feel comfortable with the whole thing. "Thanks, sir, for the invitation, but maybe some other time."

"Did I mention we pay a thousand dollars plus expenses?" I almost choke on my Dr. Pepper.

"What time should I be there?" (I already said you would think I was making this up. This was over thirty years ago when $1,000 was, well, $1,000.)

At the reception desk of the Same Name As A Cracker Hotel the nice little clerk gal wants to see my credit card. I explain to her that I don't have a credit card. In fact, I don't even have a real job. Plus, I don't see why you need a credit card in the first place—everything is paid for by the Same Name As A Cracker Hotel. The credit card, she politely explains, is for "incidentals." I politely explain that I never do anything "incidentally. Everything I do, at least at my age, is pretty much done on purpose." She makes an exception.

I like women. Married one over forty-two years ago, as a matter of fact. Like this one. But this nice little receptionist gal does not shave her armpits and I find that a tad distracting. She has the most hairy armpits of any woman I have ever seen—in my whole life. At first glance I mistakenly think she has Buckwheat in a head-lock.... (Politically incorrect? Still funny? Mildly humorous? Don't care? Will never read my stories again?)

The Same Name As A Cracker Hotel manager floats over and introduces himself. Super nice guy. Very stylishly dressed, I might add. Brando—that is his name—gives me a tour of the hotel. I suspect Brando may be engaged in an "alternative lifestyle," not that I give a fat rodent's hindquarters. I don't care. Neither should you. The only person's romantic life I have any interest in is...my own. Unfortunately, I am becoming less and less interested in that one, too. By the way, those of you who think this is some sort of subtle "slur"—I will have you know I checked with all my gay friends. He said it was fine.

Brando shows me a beautiful old antique table in the lobby. Prettiest dern table I ever saw. "That table," Brando announces proudly, "goes back to Louis the Fourteenth!" I tell my new friend Brando not to worry about it. I have a refrigerator at home that goes back to Sears on the fifteenth.

It is only early afternoon and I thought I would have a beer in the hotel saloon. Once inside I find out it isn't a saloon at all, but a "salon." A fancy haircut joint. They work me in as a walk-in. Somewhat of a special occasion for me: a walk-in and atmosphere, both the very same day.

Did I want the "works"? Shampoo, cut, style and a manicure? Of course! Especially since I am sending the bill over to the Same Name As A Cracker Hotel. Besides, I never had a manicure before. The manicurist is a pretty little twenty-something young woman who is cute as a baby mule. She sits me down at a little table and commences to work on my fingernails. Kind of like a farrier trimming hooves. Pretty soon she gets all scrunched around and her little knee inadvertently gets between my two knees.

"Sir," she says, looking up sweetly, "do you want your cuticles pushed back?"

You are going to have to write this next line yourself. I know what you are thinking.—*BJ*

> **"Did I mention we pay a thousand dollars plus expenses?" I almost choke on my Dr. Pepper.**

29

A Boy Among Men

The lie of omission.

It never occurred to me that my mother being ranch raised herself would hate living in town as much as I did. Or that she sold our little place and disposed of the livestock only because I refused to follow doctor's orders limiting my activity and hopefully preventing further damage to my polio-crippled legs.

She enrolled me at Centennial High School in Pueblo, Colorado, and gave me two dimes, two nickels and a quarter every school day. I was allowed to walk a quarter block south and catch a city bus to school. Bus fare was fifteen cents each way. The quarter was for lunch in the noisy cafeteria. There were hundreds of kids in that big school and not a ranch kid among 'em. The homeroom teacher was instructed to keep me in the building and see that I got on the city bus after school.

One Monday morning I walked a mile north to Highway 50 and caught a ride west with a fellow who called himself "Larry the Quality Roofer." He traveled around repairing roofs. We ended up three hundred miles west in Norwood, Colorado. He handed me a fistful of dollar bills and told me he had to go visit a sick sister and would pick me up in a day or two. Larry had been telling people the silver stuff he sprayed on their roofs was developed in Europe and would last twenty-five years. There was no sick sister. Larry had to hunt new country fast because an overnight rainstorm washed all the silver stuff off the roof we repaired for the Norwood Ford dealer.

I bought some quilts at the secondhand store and bedded down in a wrecked log truck parked behind the theater. When I ran out of money, Charlie let me eat three meals a day in the cafe for helping him clean up the Lone Cone Café and Bar every night after closing.

Charlie found me in the back room reading a book. He didn't like me hanging around the bar while it was open. "The big guy at the end of the bar is Tom Ritt," he said. "He can't find any help and is looking for log skidders to work mules. Maybe you ought to hit him up for a job."

Tom hired me and went right on drinking shots of Jack Daniels with beer chasers until closing time. Charlie handed me two twenty-dollar bills and told me to be careful in the woods. Tom gave me a rambling set of directions to a cabin on Lone Cone Mountain and the keys to his 1952 GMC pickup. I wondered how bad he'd be hungover.

The next morning he sat on the edge of the bunk in his long underwear, looked at me and frowned. "Get me a drink of water."

I'd approached him at an angle the night before so he could not see me in the bar mirror, but there was no way to hide my crippled leg in the one-room cabin. He scowled as I limped across the rough lumber floor with his cup of water. I had been up for an hour and

> Larry had been telling people the silver stuff he sprayed on their roofs was developed in Europe and would last twenty-five years. There was no sick sister. Larry had to hunt new country fast because an overnight rainstorm washed all the silver stuff off the roof we repaired for the Norwood Ford dealer.

A top hand with a well-trained team in good logs can skid and deck ten thousand board feet in a long day. The pay was six dollars per thousand board feet and good money in 1956. Money was split between the man and the owner of the mule. This photo was taken in North Carolina in April 1940.

filled the shiny bucket with fresh water from a beaver pond below the cabin.

"How old are you, boy? And don't lie to me."

I swallowed the always ready eighteen. "Uh, sixteen...almost."

"Oh my gawd!" Tom yelled, throwing the empty cup across the cabin. "I went and hired a crippled infant for a log skidder. That son-of-a-bitch Jack Daniels done it to me again."

I picked up the dented tin cup and hung it on a nail above the water bucket.

"You're too damn young to work in the woods. You know that, don't you?"

"Yes sir."

"Why'd you lie to me?"

"You didn't ask how old I was."

"Do you read the Bible?"

"Not much."

"Me neither, but my mother does. Do you know what a sin of omission is?"

"Kind of."

"I consider you not telling me you were fifteen years old and crippled a lie of omission. What do you think about that?"

I looked at the floor and didn't answer.

"Do you know what the law would do to me if I let you work in the woods?"

"No sir."

"I don't either, but I bet I wouldn't like it." This sober and hungover Tom was nothing like the jolly expansive fellow who hired me.

"I got logs to skid. The rest of the crew will be here today. I ain't got time to haul your ass back to town. Willie Spoo won't be here for two weeks to scale the logs and pay me. Dammit! I'm stuck with you, but you're damn sure going back to town. Can you cook?"

"Yes sir."

"Where in hell would a wet-behind-the-ears dink like you learn to cook?"

"I stayed in cow camps with my uncles. They taught me."

"Huh. Can you make pancakes?"

"Yes sir."

"Well, make some."

I had made coffee on the little tin sheepherder's stove and took him a cup. The questions kept coming while I cooked sausage, fried eggs, and pancakes.

"Do you know which end of a mule the collar goes on?"

"Yes sir."

"When did you ever harness a mule?"

"I lived with my uncle Dell one winter on the At Last Ranch at the foot of Wolf Creek Pass. We used a team and sled to feed cows."

"I know the ranch. You'd damn sure have to feed with a team in that country."

We ate our pancakes in silence. My mind wandered to something my grandpa had told me. In the trail-driving days and when big ranches still pulled a wagon out, cowboys often called their cook the Old Woman. Here I was almost sixteen, and had gone from sweeping out a bar to a two-week unpaid job as Old Woman for a log-skidding outfit. I was definitely moving up in the world.

Tom's two older brothers, Orville and Jack, showed up about noon. Orville had a couple of scruffy looking characters with bloodshot eyes with him. I figured both would end up dumped in town with me in two weeks.

"Jack," Tom said, "take this kid and show him how to feed the mules. I guess you'd just as well show him what set of harness goes to which animal and see if he can tell one mule from the other."

Jack chuckled all the way up the slope to a corral built out of smooth wire strung from tree to tree. "Kinda tickles me. You fooled old Tom. Put one over on him you did. Yes siree, I'd a sure liked to a been a fly on the wall when he woke up and got a good look at you. What happened to your leg?"

"I had polio when I was eleven. It left me with a drop foot. They operated to try and fix it but I ended up with one weak leg shorter than the other."

"Ah, that was bad. I knew several families had kids crippled with polio. You seem to get around all right. Climbed up the hill purt near good as me."

Jack showed me how much grain to feed and said to keep the bunk full of Timothy hay. "Keep the stock tank full and see the mules are all watered at the creek and given oats when we come in at noon. Be sure the stock tank is full at night. Use that five-gallon bucket and fill the fifty-five-gallon drum that's in the back of my pickup. Then you can siphon the water out of the drum into the tank with that hose over there. A mule will drink at least ten gallons of water every day. Tom is a stickler about water for his animals. Don't let him catch you with a dry tank and thirsty mules.

"I'd keep an eye on them two hon-yocks Orville brought with him. I doubt they are smart as these mules. I don't trust either one of 'em."

"I won't be around long. Tom don't like me any better than you like the guys Orville brought. I'll be sent back to town when the sawmill guy comes to scale the logs and pay everybody."

"You won't be going back to town. Tom's alright. He'll just be a little cranky 'til we get some logs piled up. Told me you had coffee ready this morning. Said it was pretty good coffee, and your pancakes was fair to middling. I 'spect he'll keep you around. There's a

In the trail-driving days and when big ranches still pulled a wagon out, cowboys often called their cook the Old Woman. Here I was almost sixteen, and had gone from sweeping out a bar to a two-week unpaid job as Old Woman for a log-skidding outfit. I was definitely moving up in the world.

fishing pole behind the seat in my pickup. If I was you, I'd catch a mess of cutthroat out of the beaver pond and cook 'em up for supper. It'd settle old Tom right down if he could sit down to a nice plate of fish after we get the new skid trails broke."

"I know how to make stovetop biscuits and brown gravy."

"Well now, if you can cook up a decent feed of trout and biscuits and gravy, I might just go to whipping on old Tom myself if he was to try and leave you in town."

Jack pointed out Mike, the big gray mule he worked, and Alex, the mule Orville worked. "Tom works those ornery little black Spanish mules as a team. They are called José and Hose-b. I never could tell one from the other. That sorrel mule following you around is Judy. She's Tom's favorite and retired. Nobody works her. Judy is usually standoffish, but she has taken a liking to you or else thinks you have an apple in your pocket. The others are just mules Tom buys every spring and hires men to work. Those mules will be sold this fall so we don't have to feed 'em all winter."

Jack and I sat on a big stump bleached gray with age and enjoyed the warm sun. The view was of Rocky Mountains at their best. Our cabin was on the edge of a small park in southwestern Colorado surrounded by steep slopes thick with timber. The trees were Engelmann spruce, Douglas fir, and a few balsam. There were patches of quaking aspens where lightning or Indian-set fires had burned themselves out long ago.

We sat quiet and listened to the mules chewing their oats and a jay squawking mad at somebody about something. I could imagine

Ute hunters waiting patiently while a bull elk sent cows and calves out first to see if it was safe to leave the timber and graze in the little park.

Jack finally spoke. "Look here, boy! You see these saw marks? This tree was felled with a crosscut. There were no damn snarling chainsaws in those days. It was all back work, quiet though, just the soft sound of man-powered steel cutting through green wood. The stump we're sitting on tells me this country was logged forty, maybe fifty years ago. Nineteen and fifteen or sixteen maybe, before either of us was born. I was born in 1917."

"Here in Colorado?"

"Naw, Oklahoma. The bank took our farm in 1935 so we headed for California and ended up stranded in New Mexico. Daddy and I found some work in the oil fields. Orville married a woman with a little reservation land south of Farmington where we winter Tom's mules."

"You sure he will let me stay?"

"Oh yeah. Tom's just fussing. He likes to think he's smarter than the rest of us. He'll pretend to be mad at you for a day or two just to get his bluff in. I think he's sort of tickled you had guts enough to pull that little stunt. Claims you sneaked up beside him and he never saw you dragging your leg. Truth is, he'd have brought you anyway. He just don't like thinking you got the best of him. Trying to fool Tom or take something he considers his is kinda like trying to grab a rabbit away from a bobcat, but he hides a good heart and is liable to turn around and give you something he needs if you need it more."

"He sure don't seem that way."

"No, and he don't intend to. Tom's like a bull snake vibrating its tail trying to scare you into thinking it's a rattlesnake. Don't let him

fool you. Just do what he asks you to and before long he'll be bragging about how clever it was to hire you."

"He don't act like he likes me much."

"Just wait, you'll see."

Jack was right. When we went to town for supplies, Tom gave me a handful of money. "Take my pickup to the feed store, get plenty of hay, and three sacks of rolled oats. Get whatever you need at the grocery store to keep us all fed for two weeks."

Tom paid off the two men Orville had brought and hired two replacements. There was no mention of my not going back to camp. Charlie said he missed me helping him clean up the place. I heard Tom tell Charlie I made better biscuits than any damn woman he ever met.

While the men were eating, I'd harness mules and when everyone was gone, there was time to sweep out the cabin, wash the dishes, and go fishing. There was no mention of wages.

Life settled into a routine. I was first up and built a fire to heat water for coffee, then fed the mules and cooked breakfast, usually pancakes, eggs and sausage. Meat was kept from spoiling in gallon mason jars wrapped in burlap and held down with rocks wired to the jars. The cold water in the beaver pond made a great refrigerator.

While the men were eating, I'd harness mules and when everyone was gone, there was time to sweep out the cabin, wash the dishes, and go fishing. There was no mention of wages. But when I tried to give Tom the cash left from shopping, he would curtly refuse to take the money. Once, it was over a hundred dollars and I worried he would accuse me of taking advantage of him while he was drinking.

Tom waved me away when I tried to give him the extra money. "What's the matter? Don't you think I know how much money I gave you? Don't you think I know how much feed costs? Don't you think I am smart enough to subtract one from the other? Next thing, you will be making me change underwear every day and

"This Old Hat"
Tack room in Bridgeport barn.
© *Calli Armstrong*

for someone to sit around reading and the rest of us don't know what's being read?"

"Seems like it to me, Jack."

"He might be reading dirty books. How would we know? I don't think we should allow reading dirty books in our camp. What would Ma say? She'd take a broomstick to the whole lot of us. Especially that kid there, reading them dirty books."

After Jack's complaining about my manners, I read to the men every night. I read Will James, "Horses I've Known," "Cowboys North and South," and "Smokey, The Cow Horse." I read books by Andy Adams, Teddy "Blue" Abbott, and Henry Herbert Knibbs. Sometimes I would go to sleep listening to the men discussing what had been read that night.

Jack had forgotten to bring his glasses and he appointed me camp scribe. Every two weeks there would be a letter from his mother for me to read out loud. Occasionally, he would dictate a reply.

Willie Spoo's check for the logs bounced and Tom had to go to Albuquerque and shake some cash out of the little crook. I asked him to stop by and pick up Jack's glasses. There were some family things in their mother's letters that should be kept private.

"What glasses? Hell, Jack can read a brand on a cow at a hundred yards. He don't have no glasses. He just don't know how to read writing. Ma tried to teach him but he never seemed to get the idea. Knows his numbers good, better than me. He just can't read, that's all. Ma knows Orville usually reads her letters to him. Orville reads better than me. He almost finished high school."

The missing glasses were never mentioned again.—*VQ*

watch my language. Stop by that dinky little library and get yourself some more books and go get our mail. Leave me alone, I am trying to have a drink and visit with Charlie."

Books became an issue because I usually read after supper until bedtime. One evening, Jack said, "Say Tom, don't you think it's rude

A Shepherd's Lament, Part I

Quit bad-mouthing watermelon and fried chicken.

Slim Atwater is a successful sheep rancher in Wyoming. By successful, I mean he "breaks even" most years and has avoided bankruptcy more than a few times. Most of his good fortune has been based on the efforts of his wife, Cherry, who is a licensed beautician and has a thriving shop in Baggs, The Best Little Hairhouse in Wyoming. Cherry has saved the ranch from foreclosure many times since Jimmy Carter was president.

Starting out with a couple dozen "bum" lambs while he was still in high school, Slim has parlayed his livestock venture into three bands of sheep that he grazes on government land with the help of some Basque shepherds. Slim's dad, a failed llama rancher, had advised Slim to avoid sheep because sheep "spend their time looking for an excuse to die." Slim learns from an early age to not give his sheep any excuse for dying. Also, to watch his flock like a starving coyote, make sure sheep and shepherds have enough to eat, and be nice to the Forest Service and Bureau of Land Management workers who control his grazing permits.

Slim was recently elected president of the Wyoming Wool Growers Association and, in what Cherry describes as a "stroke of genius," initiates a plan to get folks to eat more lamb. Slim surmises some ethnic groups eat more lamb than others—mainly Arabs, Jews and people from New York with funny-sounding last names. A subsequent huge and expensive advertising campaign is a colossal failure because in Wyoming there just aren't that many Arabs, Jews, or people from New York with funny-sounding last names.

Another campaign idea, stolen unabashedly from our beef-producing friends, has the slogan, "Mutton—a great choice for dinner!" This seemed brilliant at the time but turned out about like you would expect....

In reference to Slim's first ad campaign, a Casper newspaper reporter accuses Slim of being a racist because of his suggestion that Arabs, Jews, and folks from New York with funny-sounding last names all like lamb. Furthermore, he maintains this bigoted, prejudiced suggestion is akin to implying that all African Americans like watermelon and fried chicken. Slim replies in an emotional letter to the editor that he really doesn't even know any Jews, Arabs, or folks from New York with funny-sounding last names. Also, he only knows one African American, namely Jebediah Washington, a team roper who cowboys on a nearby ranch, and Slim states that he knows for a fact Jebediah loathes watermelon—although admittedly Jeb is somewhat reluctant about bad-mouthing the fried chicken.

The notoriety Slim obtains from these issues results in Slim being invited to a fancy dinner party hosted by an environmental group. It seems this particular organization is concerned that cattle and sheep on public land will turn the state of Wyoming into the Sahara Desert and cattle flatulence will contribute to global warming and the destruction of the ozone layer. Slim is invited to represent the sheep industry and participate in "meaningful dialogue." Several cattle ranchers are also invited, but, not so respect-

VIA INTERNET

fully, decline.

At dinner the main course is some runty little whole chicken and some undercooked green beans. (Later, Slim learns they were not chickens at all but...quail.) Wine is served but it is lukewarm and Slim asks the "wine guy" to bring him a large glass with some ice in it.

During dinner Slim has already sucked the meat off the drumsticks of what he thinks is a midget chicken and now is at a loss what to do with the bones. A perfumed and pampered little rat-faced poodle is skulking under the table—obviously the spoiled pet of the hostess. Slim's dog, Harpo, loves chicken bones and consumes them with a lot of gnawing, slobbering and obvious enjoyment. Slim, in an act of kindness, slips the two little "chicken" bones to the little dog under the table. Unfortunately, Fifi (the dog) has not experienced any kind of bone in her privileged life and immediately chokes and rolls over on her back kicking all four legs in the air like a dying cockroach. Slim springs into action and drop-kicks the little bug-eyed dog into the hallway—a distance of about thirty feet—at which time Fifi upchucks the offending bones onto the Oriental rug.

You would think, Slim considers on the drive home, that folks would be appreciative of him saving the dog's life with his canine Heimlich procedure, but nooooo, not a chance. There was a lot of screaming, crying and talk about "cruelty to animals" among the dinner guests and Slim determined maybe he should make a hasty exit. On the way home, still hungry, he stops in Farson for a Pepsi and a Mr. Goodbar.

By the time Slim reaches home he concludes, "High society just ain't what it is cracked up to be."—*BJ*

Lessons From Leo

There was damn little evidence to support my theory that I could run a ranch.

Our family's version of the "American Dream" came true when I found a good and generous fellow with more money and optimism than common sense. We bought a rundown and abandoned government-owned ranch in the San Luis Valley of Colorado. The high altitude and short growing season made the outfit suitable for alfalfa, sheep, kids and dogs.

Low livestock prices in the fifties and a decade-long drought in the sixties had driven the former owners and most of their neighbors into bankruptcy. The seventies looked more promising. Richard Nixon had just been reelected to a second term. What could go wrong?

After evicting the badger living under the porch, my wife, Arla, settled arguments over which kid got what bedroom, overruled objections to going shopping when there were old barns and tumbled-down sheds to explore, then loaded all three kids in the car and suggested I find out how many rattlesnakes per square

© JOHN BARDWELL

foot called this particular piece of paradise home before we allowed the little ones to run loose.

I sat alone in the drab kitchen knowing from years of experience that the talented woman would come home with rolls of colorful contact paper and sheer curtain material. She'd work her magic with little money and transform the dreary house into a cheerful comfortable home. I'd be hard pressed to do half as well with the blown-in irrigation ditches and sagging fences. I contemplated the heavy cast on my left leg and wondered how I'd managed to break both ankle and knee in one wreck. It was an even bet that I had bitten off more than several men with sharp teeth and two good legs could chew.

My discouraging thoughts were interrupted by a soft knock on the kitchen door. "Come on in!" I yelled. The door opened just enough so a round brown face could peek through the gap. "Hallo," the face said. "My name is Leo Gardunio.

I would be an enlightened manager. Hired men on my outfit would be treated as equals. I would invite their opinions and encourage them to participate in every important decision. Leo hated that idea. I think he considered it a gringo plot to blame him when things went wrong.

They told me you bought this place and would need lots of help."

"Well, the proverbial they are damn sure right about that. Come in, come in. I just made fresh coffee. Help yourself."

The body to match the face was a few inches over five feet tall and nearly that wide. Mr. Gardunio was built like a fireplug and just as solid. I had no idea how to interview a prospective employee, but that presented little problem because Leo proceeded to interview himself. I just listened and nodded when he made a good point.

"Some people," he said, "pay one dollar and sixty cents for an hour, but I will work for you for one dollar and fifty cents for an hour. I know about growing alfalfa and field peas and oats and barley. I know about irrigating and fixing fence. I know about sheep and goats and something about cows. I drive tractors. I will come at six o'clock every morning except Sunday when I will come after church and I will do exactly what you tell me to do."

My first executive decision was a masterpiece. I hired Leo on the spot. He stayed with our family for more than twenty years until ill health forced his retirement. Although listening carefully, I missed the key phrase in his oral resume, "I will do exactly what you tell me to do."

When he smiled at being hired, I noticed three teeth, one in the middle on top and one on each side of his lower jaw. My kids would fight over whose turn it was to present him with a toothpick after lunch. He'd go along with the joke, put the toothpick in his pocket, and say, "I will save this for later." Somewhere, I suppose,

he had a drawerful of toothpicks the kids had given him over the years.

I had worked as a ranch hand most of my life and theorized that I could run a ranch better than most of the people I'd worked for, but there was damn little evidence to support my theory. I swore that if ever given authority over anything other than horses, dogs and cows, I would be an enlightened manager. Hired men on my outfit would be treated as equals. I would invite their opinions and encourage them to participate in every important decision.

Leo hated that idea. I think he considered it a gringo plot to blame him when things went wrong. I suspected that in a former life he had attended the Wharton School of Business because he was determined to maintain a strict, almost textbook division of labor. It was clearly my responsibility to decide what to do and when to do it. He was responsible for *not* deciding and he wasn't about to let me foist my responsibility onto him, where if things went badly I could hide behind the door and claim it was all Leo's idea.

I knew which end of a cow got up first, but had never attended the birth of a lamb. Ignorance was no deterrent. I had a friend buy me a thousand head of first-year-out Columbia range ewes bred to Suffolk bucks. It did not scare me that I knew nothing of the ways of sheep. I figured we could just treat them like little woolly cows.

Sheep are not little woolly cows. It was my good fortune that Leo's people knew all about sheep, but his dogged insistence on maintaining the proper division of labor was a roadblock. Even when it was obvious that I was in over my head and some decisions were just wild guesses, asking Leo's opinion was futile.

He'd say, "Well, I don't know, Boss."

I eventually figured a way around Leo's reluctance to criticize or offer advice. Leo was a man of many uncles. These uncles cared not a fig about the proper division of labor and were happy to give me advice up to and including what style underwear I should buy.

The solution was as simple as it was elegant. If I asked Leo what a particular uncle would say, he would tell me in exquisite detail what his uncle would say we should do and why. After all, Leo's uncles were successful farmers and ranchers in their seventies and eighties. I wouldn't dare blame one of them if things went wrong. Leo, however, kept the faith and stuck stubbornly to his policy of doing exactly whatever I told him to do.

At shipping time, we would separate the lambs from their mothers. The lambs were fed alfalfa until Basil McKinley, who bought lambs for the Swift packing plant, came to sort out the fats. Basil would use his border collies to hold lambs in a corner while he moved slowly through them feeling their backs for fat and marking rejects with a grease pencil. Only ten to fifteen percent failed the fat feel. We counted 1,213 lambs to be put in our small feedlot. I told Leo to feed them ninety bales of alfalfa every morning.

Basil showed up after a few days with trucks to sort and load fat lambs. It had been a good year. We shipped eleven hundred and were left with just over a hundred head to feed.

By the time I quit laughing, here comes Leo with another load of hay. He got off the tractor and stood there with his hands on his hips like a put-upon wife annoyed with a not-too-bright husband.

One morning, while I was shaving, I heard Leo in the kitchen talking to my wife.

"Missy," he said, "we have trouble at the lamb pens."

"What's wrong?"

"Boss has not been coming over every morning to check on the lambs like he is supposed to."

"Okay, Leo," she laughed. "I will give him a good talking to and send him right over."

I had been busy with other things and there were not enough lambs left to worry about, but Leo was feeling slighted by my lack of attention. It was a good thing he was not there when I drove up because I laughed until I could barely breathe. He had stuck to his guns and done exactly what I had told him to do and fed ninety bales of our best alfalfa every day. The pile along the feed bunk was ten feet high and as wide as a house. The poor little lambs were eating as fast as they could.

By the time I quit laughing, here comes Leo with another load of hay. He got off the tractor and stood there with his hands on his hips like a put-upon wife annoyed with a not-too-bright husband.

I looked at the giant pile of hay and the lambs eating away like starving termites, and said, "Say, Leo, how about we cut back on this hay for a few days and kind of let these lambs catch up?"

Leo said, "You know, Boss, that's what I have been thinking for quite a while now."—*VQ*

"Thanks, I needed that!"

Several generations of raising livestock and feed crops in an arid environment resulted in many family stories. Vess says one good thing about being old is nobody is left to say: "The horse you learned to ride was not a well-muscled, cow-wise, steel gray with enough Hancock in him so he would try and buck you off every morning just for fun. It was an old gray mare your grandma rode down to get the mail every Monday." Vess says they are his memories and he will remember them however it suits him. Note: This is not an old gray mare, it is a blonde donkey, but Vess was used to them, too. © Carolyn Fox

"Five more miles
won't kill you...
but I might."

"Stubborn"
A muleskinner and
his mule disagree.
© Becky Blankenship

Cowboy Poetry, Oxymorons & Baxter Black

Never one to let sleeping snakes lie, I continue to dig myself deeper into a matrimonial pit.

My first exposure to cowboy poetry was years ago on the Oregon Trail in Wyoming. I had a job as the cook on a wagon train taking folks in period wagons along the original trail. The experience was just like it was in 1850—except we had ice. And Coors Light. Everything else was the same. Well, maybe not everything. We used mules instead of oxen. (Where do you find a team of oxen these days? Plus, if oxen moved any slower they would be backing up. A three-day trip would take a month and a half.) Cowboy poetry is especially meaningful when recited from memory around the light of a campfire.

One summer night Kent Stockton, a cowboy doctor from Riverton, Wyoming, came out and did a couple of poems around the fire. He recited Bruce Kiskaddon's great classic, "When They Finish Shipping Cattle in the Fall." The poem is about an old "hand" reflecting on his life in the saddle. Lost loves, friends now gone, memories both good and bad. Melancholy and sentimental. A couple of the muleskinners—hard-living and hard-drinking guys—had tears as big as horse turds rolling down their cheeks. I was hooked.

Inspired, I wrote my fist cowboy poem, "The Cook's Revenge." I

Bill and a fellow wrangler serenade the dudes after supper. Bill knows four cowboy songs, three guitar chords and "Oh! Susanna" on the harmonica. Ranch workers say that by the end of the season they can hear these songs in their sleep.

sent it to *Western Horseman* and the editor published it. If you think this is some shameless bragging on my part...well, you would be right. Everyone was suitably shocked and surprised, but nobody more than me. A disclaimer here may be appropriate—it is years before I can convince anyone to publish anything else.

Cowboy poetry, contrary to a widespread and common misconception, is not necessarily an oxymoron. (An oxymoron, you may recall, is a contradiction in terms—like military intelligence, postal service, rap music, and, my favorite of all time, mobile home estates.) It has taken cowboy poetry around one-hundred-and-fifty years to become an overnight success. In 1985 Nevada buckaroo Waddie Mitchell and folklorist Hal Cannon set up a hundred folding chairs in Elko, Nevada, and invited some local cowboys and ranchers to come share some stories and poems. They were afraid no one would show up. Well, they did show up, and continue by the thousands every year for what is now the National Cowboy Poetry Gathering. These annual "gatherings" resemble a huge family reunion—except people like one another.

Academic folks dismiss cowboy poetry as "doggerel"—trivial, poorly constructed verse of a comic or burlesque nature. Well,

Although Bill's cooking ability is minimal, the ranch is twenty-three miles from town on a gravel road and therefore the dining options for dudes are severely limited. As head wrangler, Bill maintains the job is not as glamorous as it sounds and is akin to being a groundskeeper at a large cemetery—a lot of people are under him but nobody pays him any attention. By the way, Old West tradition requires cowboy cooks to always prepare meals wearing their hats—inside or out.

in contrast to the cowboy deals, are rather sparsely attended. Maybe a couple of blue-haired ladies from the local poetry society (along with their long-faced, coerced husbands) and some freshman English lit students from the local college in desperate search of some extra credit. For the most part such affairs are akin to intellectual water boarding. In fact, I think I would rather be water boarded than be required to attend another one. Cowboy poetry is accessible, interesting, and, almost always, *fun.*

Baxter Black, cowboy poet, humorist and enter-tainer of the "agriculture masses," is a graduate of the Colorado State School of

admittedly some of it is. But other poems—for example, the late Buck Ramsey's "Anthem"—will be around for as long as there is sagebrush on the Great Plains. Paul Zarzyski (rhymes with "whiskey"), Polish rodeo cowboy poet, is a contortionist word-smith who does some bizarre and amazing things with the English language. And there are hundreds more gifted poets out there, both men and women. Kids too. Academic poetry readings,

Veterinary Medicine. Baxter maintains that the school motto is "No matter how hard you try, you can't kill them all." (I don't think this is accurate, as much of what Baxter says must be fla-vored with a barrel of salt.) Baxter says he was not very successful as a large-animal vet but did not think it was because he charged too much. Baxter charged the same fee for each animal—five dol-lars and the hide.

PHOTO COURTESY BAXTER BLACK

Baxer Black, faithful and loyal to the end; a true friend.

Some years back Baxter was scheduled to appear in a nearby Wyoming town to dispense his special brand of wit and wisdom. I asked my bride if she was interested in attending.

"Baxter Black?" she replies. "*The* Baxter Black? World-famous cowboy poet?"

"The one and only," I answer. "Baxter is a friend of mine. I know the guy." (This may be a little stretch and is akin to saying I am drinking buddies with the pope.)

"Well," she says in a tone dripping with skepticism, "I know you know him...but does he know you?"

Those of you who have been married since Moby Dick was a minnow and the Dead Sea was only sick will instantly recognize the far-reaching implication of this loaded question. On behalf of married men everywhere, I simply could not let this go unchallenged. Privately, I have a sinking feeling that perhaps my mouth has written a check that will be returned marked "insufficient funds." I had talked with Baxter Black a time or two, but that was the extent of our "friendship."

Never one to let sleeping snakes lie, I continue to dig myself deeper into a matrimonial pit. "Baxter knows me," I reply, feigning exasperation. "In fact, I will prove it to you. I will introduce you to him the night of the show."

The moment of truth arrives much too soon. Bride in tow, I wrangle my way backstage to Baxter's dressing room. My bride has a look on her face that would be a perfect illustration in Webster's Dictionary of the word "smug." I knock boldly on the door...

"Come in!" Baxter says in that distinctive voice. He is stretched out on a recliner, most probably trying to think up another poem. "Bill!" he exclaims, "so good to see you."

A side glance at my bride notes a look of genuine surprise. (To tell the truth, I was more surprised than her.) Baxter was gracious and charming—as usual. Little did he know we had (together) struck a blow for manhood everywhere. I make a mental note to use this incident as a nuclear weapon in any future relationship wars.

As for Baxter? Well, I could have kissed the man. Outrageous mustache and all.—*BJ*

It Behooves Me
Darwin Ranch, Gros Ventre Wilderness, Wyoming.
© Skip Klein

The Man of Many Uncles

Oh, thank God! I don't need a Ph.D. to water potatoes.

Our newly acquired farm in southern Colorado was located in the middle of a giant tract of land granted to Narcissus Lee and Carlos Beaubien by the government of Mexico with the provision that the grantees claim the land for Mexico, establish a town, and develop the land for farming and raising livestock. The property rights of the original settlers who came with Narcissus and Carlos were accepted and guaranteed in the Treaty of Guadalupe Hidalgo by the U.S. government.

The first and wisest move I made as working partner in our new enterprise was to hire a fellow named Leo Gardunio. One side of Leo's family came with the grantees and the other side met the grantees and contested the idea that Mexico could grant Ute land to interlopers. After a few battles, the Utes decided the high desert valley was too cold and windy to fight over and withdrew.

Leo knew how to solve most of the problems that confronted me as working partner, but considered himself a farm laborer and was reluctant to criticize or give advice. Leo thought I might hide behind the door when things went wrong and claim it was all his idea.

I finally figured out how to get around Leo's reluctance to

> One side of Leo's family came with the grantees and the other side met the grantees and contested the idea that Mexico could grant Ute land to interlopers. After a few battles, the Utes decided the high desert valley was too cold and windy to fight over and withdrew.

offer advice. He was a man of many uncles. All I had to do was ask what this or that uncle would say. Leo would then tell me in exquisite detail what we should do and why. His uncles were successful ranchers and farmers and I would not dare blame them when things went wrong.

Placido was the oldest and smallest of Leo's uncles and worked part time as a pest- and predator-control contractor for the state of Colorado to supplement income from his small farm. He would knock on my door every spring and offer to cure the prairie dogs that were running amok in a little horse pasture across from my alfalfa field.

Alonzo was the youngest and knew everything there is to know about sheep, but my favorite uncle who visited me most often was Delfino. Local legend had it that Delfino once grew the largest crop of the famous Red McClure potatoes ever grown in the San Luis Valley.

There is little doubt that my lack of experience at managing a farm and my penchant for trying any new idea I found in a farm magazine provided considerable entertainment for his cronies at their weekly poker games. Delfino was a kind man and careful to not hurt my feelings and make fun of my ideas,

San Luis Valley, Colorado. The valley lies between the 12,000-foot peaks of the Sangre de Cristo and San Juan Mountains in southern Colorado at about 8,000-foot elevation and gets less annual moisture than the Sonora Desert. July is the only reliable frost-free month. © David Muench

"Our family's happiest years were spent growing feed and livestock in this high dry and unforgiving San Luis Valley where little grows without irrigation," Vess says. "Too high, cold, and dry for most crops, an early developer's 1900s' advertisement hoping to attract settlers touted rich volcanic soil and a slogan promising 'Peas, Pigs, Potatoes and Prosperity.'" © David Muench

but he had a tell that I hope he controlled when playing poker. When Delfino thought one of my ideas too outrageous for comment, he would tug gently on his left earlobe.

One year the International Conference on Irrigation and Drainage was held in Fort Collins. I signed up to attend lectures by agricultural engineers from all over the world. It was great fun and I had lunch with a famous university professor and came up with the idea of raising a cash crop to supplement our meager farm income from sheep and alfalfa.

I came home with volumes of information on growing potatoes and armed with assurances from my newfound professor friend that he would advise me every step of the way. There was no way I could fail to grow a record crop.

Irrigation scheduling is critical for a potato crop so the professor laid out a plan that involved weekly phone calls to him with daily evapotransporations and soil moisture levels determined by a newly invented neutron hydroprobe. I was wildly enthusiastic. I had enlisted the wisdom of a tenured professor from a hundred-year-old land-grant university. A record potato crop was in the bag!

When Delfino came by for his weekly visit, I told him of my plan to grow a crop of potatoes, showed him the hydroprobe, and explained how the professor was going to help me with an irrigation schedule.

"Let me get this straight," Delfino said, tugging vigorously

There is little doubt that my lack of experience at managing a farm and my penchant for trying any new idea I found in a farm magazine provided considerable entertainment for his cronies at their weekly poker games. Delfino was a kind man and careful to not hurt my feelings and make fun of my ideas, but he had a tell that I hope he controlled when playing poker.

on his left earlobe. "You are going to let a professor in Fort Collins tell you when to irrigate your potatoes?"

"Right," I said.

"Why don't you just ask the potatoes?"

"Because I don't speak potato."

Delfino barely smiled at my little joke and said: "Plants and animals don't talk except in cartoons, but they speak to wise farmers in sign language. When a bull starts pawing dirt and blowing snot, he is saying, 'You are too close.' When a normally timid ewe stands her ground between you and newborn lambs then stamps her front feet at you, she is plainly saying: 'I am afraid you will hurt my babies. Go away.'

"Look at your potatoes when the day is hottest. You will see the leaves turned to protect themselves from the sun. Go back one hour before dark and you will see the leaves turned back ready for the morning sun. If the leaves turn back, do not water your potatoes. If the leaves do not turn back by dark, it is time to water your potatoes. If the leaves have not turned back by morning, you are late with your water and will have only small potatoes and not very many of those. It is like magic. The roots, somehow, take water and food from the soil. The leaves take something from the sun and together they make big beautiful potatoes.

"You see, the leaves know more about making potatoes than professors do."—*VQ*

Double Duty

Double Dutch
Skipping rope, the cowboy way.
Ira, Joe and Josh Wines at the Ira Wines Ranch in Ruby Valley, Nevada. © Kim Jackson

Double Cool

Having fun, the cowgirl way.
Gemma (the photographer's granddaughter) loves to play with the hose in
Winnemucca, Nevada, especially when she can get soaking wet! © Delia Nuffer

Gambling, Rambling, Ranching & Rehab

Are six bred heifers a herd?

I never got into the livestock business to make a lot of money. (So far, that part has worked out better than I ever expected.) In 1988, I purchased my first herd of cattle: six bred heifers. Can you call six heifers a herd? Good question. I asked the Wyoming rancher I bought them from this same thing. "Well," he replied sagely, "once your check clears you can call them any damn thing you want."

A year or so later I sold them and made a little money. Perhaps I should have quit while I was ahead. But this event was like a degenerate gambler winning a jackpot on his first pull of a slot machine. It is here that the first seeds of unreal expectations and borderline fanaticism were inadvertently sewn. Quit? What if I had a hundred heifers? Or a thousand? Then I could buy a new dually pickup, an airplane and, eventually, the King Ranch down in Texas. It is this type of illogical, magical thinking that built Las Vegas. Somebody, after all, must pay for those beautiful fountains, lights and "free" whiskey.

Some of you may wonder where I am going with this analogy. Be patient. We are getting there eventually. I have been visiting Vegas for forty years, and although I don't gamble much anymore—raising cattle has satisfied any urges I previously had concerning risking it all—there are a lot of parallels related to ranching/farming, livestock production, and degenerate gambling. There is a saying among card-playing gamblers that goes something like this: When you first sit down at a poker table, look around. If you can't immediately identify the sucker there, guess what? The sucker is you. Over the last thirty years or so I have had the same feeling when picking up a less-than-adequate check at the sale barn. "Perhaps," I have thought many times, "the sucker is me."

Las Vegas, like ranching, has changed a lot in the last forty years. Big corporations have taken over almost all the casinos with alleged "mob" connections. Many others, like the Stardust, Riviera, Dunes, Frontier and Landmark, have been imploded. Blown to smithereens. Of what remains, now that the accountants and tax lawyers are in charge, I am certain no financial hijinks are taking place. (I will pause here as I attempt to remove my tongue from my cheek. By the way, I liked Vegas a lot better when the other guys ran the place.)

Ranching/farming, et cetera, is now "agribusiness." Comparisons? I will leave that up to you. One thing is for sure though. In Vegas, the days of the ninety-nine-cent breakfast are long gone.

Last year I picked up a little pamphlet from Gamblers Anonymous. "Do you have a gambling problem? Answer these questions to find out." I took the liberty of substituting "ranching" for "gambling."

- *"While ranching, have you often found yourself in financial distress?"*
- *"Have you ever borrowed money so you could continue ranching?"*
- *"Has ranching ever interfered with your personal relationships?"*
- *"Have you, while ranching, ever found yourself chasing your losses?"*
- *"Do you continue ranching believing your bad luck is due to change?"*

What if I had a hundred heifers? Or a thousand? Then I could buy a new dually pickup, an airplane and, eventually, the King Ranch down in Texas. It is this type of illogical, magical thinking that built Las Vegas.

A young heifer thinks about the future at the Levaggi Ranch in Amador County, California. © *Carolyn Fox*

Anyway, you get the idea. A rancher friend of mine who considers himself a good poker player went to Vegas and promptly lost $10,000. A call to his banker for more money was met with no resistance. On his return to the ranch he stopped to look at a new pedigreed herd bull. He called his banker for another $10,000. "Can't do it," the banker said. "Too risky. I would rather invest in a school of fish off the coast of Cape Cod." I wish I was making this up.

There is an old joke—unfortunately much too true to be very funny—about a rancher who was asked, "What would you do with a million dollars?" You already know his answer. "I would just keep ranching till it was all gone."

As for me, I think I will just give up on the whole cattle-raising venture. But then again, cattle prices look like they might be on the way up. The new calves are all thriving and there is plenty of grass. Maybe I will try one more year.... My luck is bound to change.—*BJ*

Pocket Gopher Stew

Tales from Stuttering Bill. As told to Vess Quinlan.

Finding Stuttering Bill working nights as a New Mexico Port of Entry officer in Clayton was a great surprise and made me look forward to the weekly trips hauling alfalfa to Texas from our little outfit in the San Luis Valley of Colorado. Bill was a great storyteller and after telling me his version of my turkey-fighting summer with my Uncle Dell and Aunt Helen on the Red Top Ranch east of Walsenburg, Colorado, Bill would have a new story ready whenever I walked in the little scale house.

"I don't guess I ever told you how I come to be called Stuttering Bill."
"No. You never did."

Well...my folks was blown out of the Panhandle of Oklahoma during the Dust Bowl, along with a lot of other good folks, when I was nine years old. My dad was a good man, well thought of and a hell of a hand with a horse. His specialty was starting colts for work teams. Some of them big devils was four or five years old and never been touched. Had Percheron fighting blood in 'em. My dad could sweet talk those rowdy giants into being gentle willing workhorses.

Most field work was done with horses. Oh, there were a few tractors around, most of 'em setting broke down in the middle of some field. Horses were more reliable and a lot quieter. I never took to the tractor idea myself. I didn't think they would ever amount to anything.

We hung on for a few years watching our crops blow out. Sold off or ate what cattle we had. Finally got down to living off the butter and eggs my mother could sell or trade in town and what day work my dad could find with his team, Ike and Zeke, but there were few people could afford to hire him.

He went to the bank to borrow on the place and get in one more crop, but the bank turned him down. Dad got home just before dark, put his horse up and came in the house. I was studying my lessons so I would not look a fool at school the next day. I liked school, but wasn't very good at it. I jumped up and said I'd go feed the horses. We had a great big barn with a hayloft. I liked forking hay through the big square holes cut above the mangers.

Dad told me to keep at my lessons and he would feed the horses. When he did not come in to supper, mother sent me to find him. He had thrown a rope over a rafter and stepped off into one of the holes above the manger. I saw his feet hanging between Ike and Zeke.

"Come out here and see what I found. This perfectly good boy was running loose down by the river. He is pretty close to what we been hoping for. Can we keep him?"

The good folks in Oklahoma gathered around and helped every way they could, but my poor mother was left with two little girls, one three and one five, and a nine-year-old for man of the house. She did the best she could, but when an odd-job man named Ted asked her to marry him and head for California, she decided it was the only way we could stay together as a family.

Ted sawed off the tongue of one of my dad's wagons and made a hitch for his old Dodge Brothers truck. We traded our milk cow for two milk goats, loaded the goats, five of my mother's laying hens, some hay, a few sacks of grain, and headed for California.

Ted was not a good man. He was a liar and a thief. Sometimes

© JOHN BARDWELL

we would find work to buy gas for the old truck, but most of the time Ted would siphon gas out of some other person's truck or steal it out of a tractor left in the field. He sharpened a steel rod and showed me how to kick the little mound of dirt away from a pocket gopher's hole and when the gopher came to push dirt up from his hole and rebuild the mound, I'd see where the dirt was moving and stab him with the sharp rod. The meat went in a stew Mother made with whatever we could beg or steal from someone's garden. It was slow going pulling that farm wagon. We'd be lucky to make twenty miles a day. Most folks was kind but there were so many people coming through begging or stealing stuff that none of us were really welcome.

We camped along the Huerfano River in southern Colorado one night, nearly out of gas and short on food. Ted sent me out to catch some gophers for a stew. I walked for miles but there were no fresh gopher mounds. Maybe some disease wiped them out. When I walked in to camp, Ted cussed me for being a lazy good for nothing and said if I did not find some gophers tomorrow to not bother coming back.

Before I went to sleep that night, I heard Ted and my mother arguing. The next morning my mother could barely see out of her left eye. The whole side of her face was black and blue. My mother said Ted had gone up the river looking for a place to buy some gas. She lied again and said her bruises came from tripping and falling against the wagon box. That's when I decided to kill Ted. I figured to use my gopher killing rod and didn't think I'd feel any worse than I felt stabbing the ugly little pocket gophers.

Ted came back with a few gallons of gas he had stolen someplace and sent me to find gophers. I got back to camp in late afternoon and they were gone. My mother left a note between two rocks. She had no choice but to go on with Ted and try to take care of the girls. "Your dad," she wrote, "was a good kind man. You are a

That Greasy, Foul-Tasting, Pocket Gopher Stew Sounds Yummy!
Is that fresh manure ready for me to roll in at the Levaggi Ranch in the Sierra Nevada Foothills of California? © *Larry Angier*

strong boy and can make your own way. Please forgive your father and remember him kindly. Do not forget me. I love you and will think of you every day."

I did not know what to do or which way to walk, so I just sat on the rock reading my mother's note over and over until the sound of a horse's steel shoes striking rocks along the river warned me that someone was coming. There was no place to hide so I just sat there.

The rider folded his hands across the saddle horn, looked down at me and said, "Well, well, old horse, we come looking for wild cows and found a wild boy. I don't see no earmark or a brand on him so he must be a stray."

I was in no mood for jokes so I never said anything and just kept looking at the ground.

"I saw you set up camp a day or two ago. Last night the dogs started raising hell. I thought it was just coyotes getting too close, but this morning I saw man tracks where your dad had siphoned some gas out of my truck."

"He is not my dad!" I yelled. "My dad was a good man. An honest man. He would never steal your gas."

The big man got down and sat beside me on the rock.

"They left you didn't they?"

My throat swelled shut and I could not answer so I just handed him my mother's note.

"Well this is my lucky day. I am in a bind. There is a little ranch house a mile or two north of here where I live surrounded by women. There is my wife, Annie, and twin four-year-old daughters. I have been hoping a boy something like you would show up and help me even things up a little."

He stepped back on his horse then pulled his foot out of the left stirrup and held out his hand. When I reached up to take his hand, he lifted me high enough to get my foot in the stirrup so I could set behind him.

"Old Buzzard," he said, "might object to carrying double, but if I keep his head up, he can't buck us both off."

I was glad to set behind the saddle so he could not see the tears, but I think Charley knew because he talked all the way home about how much help I would be around the ranch.

That is how I met Charley Comstock.

When we got to the house, Charley hollered at Annie: "Come out here and see what I found. This perfectly good boy was running loose down by the river. He is pretty close to what we been hoping for. Can we keep him?"

The first words Annie said to me were, "Are you hungry?"

The girls wanted to know my name and why I talked funny. I told them my name was Bill and that I stuttered. Sally was shy, but Linda was outgoing and feisty. Linda put her hands on her hips, frowned, and said, "Is this true?" She was used to her dad making up outrageous stories to tease her.

Charley nodded and said: "It's true. Lots of people stutter."

Linda said: "I have a friend in Sunday school named Bill who giggles in church. We can't have two just Bills. No one will know which Bill I am talking about. So I will call him Giggling Bill and you will be Stuttering Bill."

The girls were amazed that I did not stutter when reading their little books to them or when I sang in church. I don't stutter much anymore, but I have been Stuttering Bill ever since.

Charley made me go to school and when I graduated high school offered to pay for college, but I refused and said all the education I wanted or would ever need was right there on that ranch.

I never got rich, but Charley helped me get a little ranch of my own and I gathered up a few good cows over the years. This night job with the state helps me support 'em and I've never had to choke down another bowl of greasy, foul-tasting, pocket gopher stew.—VQ

Confessions of a Capitalist Pig

Watch out for the tax man with his grubby little hand out.

A few decades ago I had a summer job riding a longhorn steer through the streets of Aspen, Colorado, as advertisement for a western clothing store. For those of you who have never been there, Aspen is the place where rich people believe they go when they die. They go there to ski in the winter, be overcharged for everything they buy, and to act like self-absorbed obnoxious movie stars. Which, of course, some of them really are.

Once you spend a little time in Aspen it is common to come up with two observations: One, there are many people in this country with entirely too much money; and two, how can I get some of it?

At one time, I even thought of getting a job in town myself, but thankfully the feeling passed quickly.

Another rather surprising thing I learn there is that most Americans have no earthly idea where the food they eat originates. Hamburger comes in those plastic-wrapped packages at the grocery store. Milk, cheese and ice cream come straight from the dairy department. Produce? Fruits and veggies have their own little section.

One morning riding my big steer down a busy street a young attractive woman comes running up to me. "What do you think you are doing?" she demands indignantly. "Can't you see that cow doesn't like this?" By the way, she has on a Harvard sweatshirt.

The Capitalist Pig (Bill, not the steer) says, "Capitalism is the worst system in the world—until you compare it with everything else."

COURTESY BILL JONES

60

Aspen is the place where rich people believe they go when they die. They go there to ski in the winter, be overcharged for everything they buy, and to act like self-absorbed obnoxious movie stars. Which, of course, some of them really are.

Right about now I know many of you are thinking, "I bet he is just making this part up." Okay...it wasn't Harvard. It was UCLA.

The little Aspen gig is an epiphany for me. I decide to become a Capitalist Pig. (I just realized there may be a cowboy poem here. "Gig" and "pig." Two rhymes already!) My plan is to return to Wyoming, buy some bred heifers, parlay them into a huge herd, then buy a Lear jet and return to Aspen as a cattle baron, walk arrogantly around with a gigantic sense of entitlement, and act snotty toward the "help." After thirty years it hasn't quite worked out this way. A little sympathy here would be appropriate. Feel my pain.

It is difficult to be a farmer/rancher and a Capitalist Pig at the same time. Every successful rancher, it has been said, has a wife who works in town. Now, with cattle prices in freefall, the little gal needs at least two jobs. At one time, I even thought of getting a job in town myself, but thankfully the feeling passed quickly. (I had a full-time job once and I didn't like it. Too many folks telling me what to do. They're called "bosses.") A lot of stockmen, many of them infinitely smarter than me, have gone broke in the sheep and

cattle industry. Too many variables over which they have absolutely no control; tough business where money making often takes a backseat to survival.

If you are fortunate enough in some years to make a little money, the tax man appears with his grubby little hand out for his share. With no investment, no risk, and certainly no work, he

Aspen Square Condominium Hotel

61

rather rudely demands a healthy portion of your profits. And he will get it, too. One way or the other. I try to use the "tax avoidance system," which means taking every legal deduction ever devised. This is in contrast to the "tax evasion system," which often results in you scarfing down your mashed potatoes off a silver-colored tray at the Atlanta Federal Penitentiary.

Capitalism gives livestock producers the right to save and buy a small farm or ranch, work forty years with no vacations, buy some adjoining land at inflated prices, and after dying from a stress-related heart attack, leave everything to their kids to squabble over in litigation for years to come. Then, after the place is sold by court order, what the lawyers don't get is bought by a real estate developer who turns the forty acres that remain into a mobile home park. Only in America. What a country!

Do you think you are getting your money's worth with the taxes you pay? Well, maybe. Capitalism is the worst system in the world—until you compare it to everything else. I would not like raising livestock in Russia, China, or Cuba. Neither would you. There the government takes it all at once. Personally, I take the following approach to taxes: Don't tax me. Don't tax you. Tax that fellow behind that tree...

How do small-time livestock producers afford health insurance? Just wondering. Me and my bride don't pay much for our health

"Lawyers occasionally stumble over the truth, but most of them pick themselves up and hurry off as if nothing happened."

WINSTON CHURCHILL (1874-1965),
SELDOM SEEN IN ASPEN BECAUSE HE WAS TOO BUSY
AND THE LAWYERS WERE ALREADY THERE

insurance. We have Medicare. All you folks out there under sixty-five years of age are footing our health-care expenses. Thanks. I know the country is broke and more than twenty trillion in debt, but I don't care. Keep paying those doctor bills! If I were you, though, I would be somewhat resentful about paying for health care for the guy with no job, a hundred pounds overweight, smoking two packs of cigarettes a day, sleeve tattoos, the latest cell phone, cable with all the premium channels, rings in several soft-tissue body parts, and no intention of trying to improve his condition. Or *ever* getting a job. But maybe that's just me.

Back to Aspen. I have been wandering off the trail like a one-eyed longhorn. While I was riding a steer around getting abused by yuppies, my folks (long gone now) flew out to see me. My dad was a small-time capitalist in his own right. Starting with fifty gumball machines, he built his business into a successful company with fifteen employees. Only in America. What a country! Anyway, the first morning Dad went out and purchased a couple of coffees and two brownies. The bill was almost fifty bucks. This event was the absolute highlight of his trip. He kept the receipt and talked about it for the rest of his life. "Best damn brownie I ever ate," Dad said. "I even tipped the guy five bucks. They don't like cheapskates in Aspen."

You can say that again.—*BJ*

Under the Big Sky

Sitting on the pairs and waiting for them to mother up, my faithful partner, Roxy, always by my side and the horses, Tantrum and Bonnie, enjoying a bite to eat at the Hat Creek Ranch in Wisdom, Montana. © Danielle Coon

New Boots for Bob

A gift from Santa.

Clyde carefully rolled a fresh Prince Albert cigarette. The cigarette could have been mistaken for a tailor-made except for a slight hump in the middle. He eyed me for a moment and said: "I might've guessed you were Bob's boy even if Grandma Williams had not told me your name. You look a lot like your dad."

"Where did you meet my dad?"

"Well now. Let's see. It would have been thirty-four years ago this spring. Your dad's oldest sister, Mary, had married Fred Rule. Fred was cowboss for Sloss Brothers up the Frying Pan River out of Basalt, Colorado. I had been starting colts, chasing cows around, fixing fence, washing windows and one thing or another on the Sloss Brothers outfit for several years.

"Your dad's mother died in nineteen and twenty-five. I believe he was almost six when your grandfather, Emmett, brought him to live with Fred and Mary. I did not know your grandfather, but I heard he never amounted to much. He would not stay home and look after his

© JOHN BARDWELL

family. The story is your grandmother worked herself to death washing clothes and cleaning rich folks' houses to support the family. There was Mary, Florence, Walt and your dad. Your dad was the youngest. The others were grown and married.

"I guess your grandfather had enough of a conscience to feel bad about dumping a small boy on a newly married older sister. In any event, he took your dad to the general store in Eagle before he brought him to the ranch and bought him a brand new pair of red cowboy boots.

"Your dad put a new mark on being poor. All he had with him was a faded flour sack with a few patched clothes, a smelly old corncob pipe he found somewhere and would not part with, and the new red boots his dad bought him. When the lady store clerk guessed at what size boots would fit and brought the shiny new pair for your dad to try on, he thought the store only had one pair and was afraid if he admitted they hurt his feet, he would not get new boots.

"It did not take long to figure out why the little

64

"Well I'll be damned! I thought I heard something last night, but thought it was just that old pack rat looking for something to steal."

fellow was limping around, but he insisted the new boots fit just fine.

"One morning, your dad was watching us unload a stack of sacked oats to feed the horses when Edgar Lippincott, who worked part-time delivering for the feed store, noticed your dad hobbling around in his new boots.

"'Them new boots is hurting your feet, ain't they boy?' Edgar said. 'Well I know how to fix that. One time my cousin Elmer gave me a pair of boots he had outgrown. He was a year older than me, but I was growing faster than him so the boots hurt my feet just like those boots are hurting yours. My daddy knew how to fix them. He soaked some oats and poured them in the boots. When the oats swelled up they stretched the boots so they fit perfect. I wore them boots to school all year long.'

"Now," Clyde continued, "Edgar was one of those fellows who knows a little something about everything and not much about anything, but he could be real persuasive and it sounded like it might work. So we put some oats to soak while we finished unloading the truck. Edgar packed the new boots with oats and said if we set them behind the stove in the bunkhouse all night that by morning they would fit your dad just right.

"I had just finished shaving when your dad busted into the bunkhouse at daylight the next morning to try on his boots. The oats had swelled up alright, but Edgar had apparently packed too many oats too tight in the little boots. Your dad's new boots were ruined; every seam was split wide open. He tried hard not to cry, but finally lost the battle and broke down sobbing. I wanted to take him on my lap and hold him, but was afraid he would not let me so I just sat there beside him on my bunk while he held the little boots and cried.

"When the crying stopped, I said, 'It's not long until Christmas. Maybe Santa Claus will bring you a pair of boots that fit.'

"'I don't believe in Santa Claus,' he said.

"We had a little Christmas tree in the bunkhouse and when your dad came in on Christmas morning, he stopped still and stared at the brand new pair of little red cowboy boots under the tree.

"'Well I'll be damned,' I said. 'I thought I heard something last night, but thought it was just that old pack rat looking for something to steal and here it was Santa Claus leaving your new boots.'

"The new boots fit perfect. Your dad looked at me for a long time, then said: 'I don't think Santa Claus brought these boots. I think you bought them when you went to town last week. Thank you, Mr. Sweeney.'

"I looked your dad right in the eye and said, 'Well, you can believe whatever you want, but I believe in Santa Claus and I always will.'"—VQ

The Bridge to "No Where"

This bridge, located approximately sixteen miles south of the Idaho border, crosses the Owyhee River in northeastern Nevada's high, dry back country. The boundless desolation of the area contains a whole lot more animals than people.

The bridge was initially intended to cross the river to access a landfill, but that dream never happened. Today, it crosses the river and connects to a dirt road that just ends. Stops. Disappears. Now some might consider that to be "some where."
Photos © Larry Angier

A Shepherd's Lament, Part II

Lowering standards at the Dew Drop Inn Café & Bar.

On his way back from Rock Springs, Wyoming, with a stock trailer full of "open" ewes, Slim Atwater decides to stop at the Dew Drop Inn Café & Bar before returning to the ranch. He figures he made enough from the ewes to pay for his gas and a couple of beers before going home. Slim, a sheep rancher near Baggs, has recently been removed from his position as president of the Wyoming Woolgrowers Association after his brainchild advertising campaign—"Eat More

Curious leppy lambs at the Dufurrena Ranch in Nevada. © Larry Angier

Mutton"—is a miserable and gargantuan flop. Slim, after thirty years in the sheep-raising business, and therefore very accustomed to failure, takes the attitude, "Well, you can't win 'em all."

Slim's wife, Cherry, owner of The Best Little Hairhouse in Wyoming, has gone to Rawlins to visit her brother, Harry R. Balls, also formerly of Baggs, who is now doing three to five in the Wyoming State Penitentiary for bank fraud. It seems Harry had some cows on his place just outside of Baggs and was supplementing his income with a muffler shop in town. What Harry failed to realize, until much too late, is that folks in Baggs and the sur-

rounding county do not replace a vehicle's muffler until it rusts out and falls off. Harry applies for a business loan and "exaggerates" the value of assets he owns and uses these inflated and phantom assets for collateral. He submits (per a legal affidavit) that he owns one hundred and fifty cows instead of the twenty-four he really does own. Also, he lists a bunch of farm equipment that does not exist. At least not on *his* ranch.

At Harry's sentencing hearing the judge notes that investigation reveals Harry owns only one piece of farm equipment—a 1950 8N Ford tractor—which doesn't run and has no seat or steering wheel. In an effort to introduce some levity to the situation Harry tells the judge that it is perfectly appropriate the tractor has no seat or steering wheel, "because I have lost my ass and have nowhere to turn." The judge, a humorless man by all accounts, gives Harry an additional six months. "Perhaps, Mr. Balls," the judge reflects, "you do not know the seriousness of bank fraud. Even I know a junk tractor is not worth $22,000."

Slim, stopping at the aforementioned Dew Drop Inn, notes it is Friday night and the place is somewhat crowded. One of Cherry's contract employees, a hair stylist named Juanita Duffleberg, an immigrant from somewhere back East, is chatting up a couple of ranch hands from the Double Zero Ranch. Juanita, a skilled beautician who specializes in the infamous beehive hairdo, likes men. All men. Unfortunately, pickings are slim around Baggs, the whole county being populated by broke cowboys and struggling, married and depressed ranchers. A girl just can't get a break these days and Juanita has already lowered her standards more than she ever intended.

It is rare to find any man within two hundred miles of Baggs, Juanita complains, "who will even buy a lady a drink." Indeed, it looks like another boring Friday evening at the Dew Drop until Juanita spies Slim. Juanita knows Slim because he stops by the beauty shop four or five times a week to "borrow" money. Maybe Slim has enough pocket change to buy her a beer. Maybe even two. Hope, like pasture weeds and cowboy poets, springs eternal.

"Where is Cherry?" Juanita asks Slim. On being told Cherry is out of town and will not be home till later, Juanita lights up like a Japanese pinball machine. "Would you like to dance?" she asks, batting her eyes rapidly like a cow with pinkeye. Slim explains that he does not dance much, although after a pack or so of Schlitz Malt Liquor he can do an acceptable rendition of the "Hillbilly Stomp." About this time Slim's favorite song comes on the jukebox, "Thank God and Greyhound She's Gone." Unable to resist, Slim allows Juanita to pull him onto the dance floor where she proceeds

Juanita lights up like a Japanese pinball machine. "Would you like to dance?" she asks, batting her eyes rapidly like a cow with pinkeye. Slim explains that he does not dance much, although after a pack or so of Schlitz Malt Liquor he can do an acceptable rendition of "Hillbilly Stomp."

to wrap around him like a vine on a rotting fence post. It is at this point in our story that things take what could be considered an ugly turn.

Cherry has cut short her prison visit with Harry in Rawlins as she wants to attend a Tupperware party at a friend's house on the way home. After that event she spies Slim's truck and stock trailer in the parking lot of the Dew Drop and decides to stop and show him what she bought at the party. Upon entering the dimly lit bar she sees what she thinks is one person on the dance floor. Soon enough Cherry realizes it is Slim and Juanita dancing so close together a communion wafer would not fit between them.

Enraged, and much to the amusement of the other bar patrons, Cherry pulls the two apart and begins beating Slim about the head and shoulders with one of those plastic popsicle trays. Later all the customers say this was the most entertaining event that ever happened at the Dew Drop Inn, with the possible exception of the time two fat gals got in a wrestling match in the parking lot over the results of a wet T-shirt contest.

Later, Slim and Cherry decide this one minor incident is not cause for a divorce. Juanita returns to civilization, where folks appreciate her hair "artistry" and all the men are not continually broke. Slim is relieved because The Best Little Hairhouse in Wyoming is keeping their ranch operation from bankruptcy. Cherry decides Slim has a few less faults than any other man she has known. And, down deep where it counts, she really does kind of like the guy—even though most of the time he smells like sheep.—*BJ*

The Lost Bull

Closer than you think.

When I pulled across the scales at the Clayton Port of Entry in New Mexico, I could see Stuttering Bill sitting on his little stool with head down on folded arms appearing to be sound asleep. I did not want to embarrass him by catching him sleeping on the job, so I made a big production of kicking imaginary snow off my boots before entering. Bill slept on. I slammed the door hard from the outside and reentered.

"Damn," Stuttering Bill said, "I'm sure glad it's you. It's pretty hard to get fired off a state job and I need this night work to support my little herd of cows, but a supervisor catching you asleep will get anyone fired. I'm wore out from working here all night and spending all day horseback for a week looking for my new bull."

"Did you find him?"

"Yes, and not a hundred yards from the house."

"Was he alive?"

"He was alive alright and it's a good thing too. I decided to buy a registered bull from Banning and Lewis to try and wean a little heavier calves. I went in to visit my banker and ask for a loan to buy a better bull. That banker studied my file for a long time and after a lot of frowning, he said he'd loan me the money. I was told to write a check to pay for the bull and come in when I got the bull home and settled to sign the loan papers so they could cover the check when it came in. If you think that banker frowned over my file, you should have seen him frown when I told him how much I paid for that bull. I was afraid he was going to ruin his forehead and end up with permanent frown lines. I will admit that I got carried away and spent more than I should have, but I just fell in love with that bull and had to have him."

Bill continued: "I put my new bull in the little horse pasture and fed him my best alfalfa and a little grain every morning so he'd be happy in his new home. When that big storm blew in last week, that bull disappeared from the little pasture. I rode my country and all my neighbors' country looking for that bull, but he was nowhere to be found. There was a strong wind with that storm and it piled up big drifts. I was afraid he had gotten down in one of the draws and smothered under a snowdrift.

"This morning, I was standing out on my back porch wondering how I was going to tell that banker his collateral had flown the coop, so to speak. I doubted he would loan me any more money to buy another bull since I did not take very good care of the one I just bought. Then I heard what sounded like boards breaking in a little shed I used for storing sacks of cottonseed cake, when I could afford to buy any. I seen a lot of lion track when I was hunting that bull so I figured one of those big cats had gotten itself trapped in the little shed.

"Snow had drifted up against the shed and the wind had blown off most of the shingles. I got my rifle and sneaked up the drift where I could look through the roof into the shed and there was my bull looking up at me. I suppose the wind had blown the door open and he went in and managed to close the door on himself so he could not get out. He had walked around packing the snow that blew into the shed until he was breaking the rafters with his horns. I thought about shooting him.

"I said: 'You big dddummy! Why didn't you say something? One little bbeller would have been enough.'"—*VQ*

Always Looking for a Date
The season with the girls is over and this bull in Hell's Corner, Montana, is not happy about that. © Cynthia Baldauf

Ranching, Goat Yoga & Financial Freedom

If you think the Praying Cow Pose is difficult, try doing it with a goat standing on your back.

Since my bride has been involved in the latest exercise craze I have learned more about yoga than I really wanted to know. Although she has encouraged me to join her, I have declined in that I avoid pain and potential humiliation at every opportunity. There are several yoga positions I *have* learned about from watching her practice:

"The Praying Cow Pose." I have seen a lot of cows, maybe millions over a lifetime, but have yet to see one pray.

"The Peeing Dog Pose." As opposed to the Praying Cow, I have witnessed lots of dogs peeing. A blue heeler I once had would pee every thirty minutes on any stationary object available.

"The Plank With Sag in the Middle Pose." Why anyone would want to use a warped board is beyond me...

"The Stork Standing on One Leg With Balance Issues Pose." This one is self-explanatory.

"The Corpse in a Coffin Pose." This is the only pose I think I could probably be good at.

Also, there is more to this yoga thing than meets the eye. It is necessary to buy special clothes called yoga pants that are the required uniform of the day. My wife has several dozen pair. Everywhere I go I see women wearing these things, some who obviously have never been to a yoga class in their lives. Just because these are "stretch pants," there is no need to try and get your 250-pound rear end into a pair. Just saying. For those of you who are thinking I am a sexist pig, this same advice goes for all my beer-gutted yoga guys out there. Keep your lard butts out of the yoga pants.

Yoga, from what I can gather, has a philosophy that goes along with the semicontortionist and partially obscene exercise routines. It is called "mindfulness." The past is gone, the future is unknown, and all you have is *now*. Think about what you are doing while you

Just because these are "stretch pants," there is no need to try and get your 250-pound rear end into a pair.

are doing it. For example, if you are riding along on your horse and it unexpectantly humps up and commences to buck, you should already have picked out a soft place to land. More than that, though, it should have crossed your mind that—at least at your age—maybe you should never have gotten on the half-broke SOB in the first place.

This part I know you will think I am just making up, but I saw it on cable TV, so it must be true. These yoga folks are doing the above-mentioned poses with pygmy goats. Really! If you think the Praying Cow Pose is difficult, try doing it with a goat standing on your back. (If any male goats are being used I hope they have been neutered, otherwise some unpleasant scenarios could...well, we won't go there.) This whole weird situation has given me some great life-changing, money-generating ideas. Bear with me on this...

If the whole goat-yoga thing continues to grow, the demand for goats will grow and multiply. Every yoga enthusiast will need their own private pygmy goat. Maybe two. We are talking potentially millions of goats here, folks. No doubt goat prices will rise and up to $100 per goat is not out of the question. Now for the unbelievable "financial opportunity" part: If a guy has a ranch/farm that supports seventy-five or so momma cows, that very same place could well handle about 15,000 pygmy goats. Plus, they don't eat much and are happy just munching on weeds. Counting twin births, that is 15,000 baby pygmy goats a year! In a particularly bad winter a

From left: Granddaughter Leah Jones, age ten, in yoga pose without goat; Bill Jones, age seventy, in semi-yoga pose with uncooperative family cat (goat unavailable); and Gloria Jones, age seventy, in yoga pose with family cat substituting for pygmy goat.

couple of pickup loads of hay from the local co-op should carry you through without much trouble. Or you could rent the goats out as four-legged Russian thistle, weed and kudzu eliminators. Or turn your farm/ranch temporarily into the world's largest petting zoo. The possibilities are endless. As you can probably ascertain by now, I have given a lot of serious thought to this project.

We are talking $1,500,000 a year. (Or is it $150,000? Whatever, it is more than you are making with those seventy-five cows.) This

plan could revolutionize the entire livestock industry.

What, you may ask, if this whole goat-yoga thing is a passing fad and the bottom drops out of the yoga pygmy goat market? Don't think I have not thought about that and have a foolproof backup alternative. It is the Barbeque Goat Meat plan. Our friends down in Mexico eat a lot of goats, as well as folks in the Middle East. (Some we don't like but, after all, this is strictly business and sacrifices must be made.) To be truthful, I have only eaten goat

To be truthful, I have only eaten goat meat one time—down in Mexico. Unfortunately, it was the same occasion I was introduced to tequila, and there was an unfortunate episode with a couple of "señoritas" who, it turned out, were not really señoritas at all.

meat one time—down in Mexico. Unfortunately, it was the same occasion I was introduced to tequila, and there was an unfortunate episode with a couple of "señoritas" who, it turned out, were not really señoritas at all, plus an attempted bullfight with a donkey pulling a cartful of fruit. (I am embarrassed to say the donkey won.) A 500 peso bill to the local cop prevented an overnight stay in the local El Cross Bar Hotel. A potentially unpleasant situation. Did the goat meat taste like chicken? I wish I could remember.

Some of you more cynical ranchers/farmers may be asking what is my "hook" on this miraculous and near-genius route to financial independence. All I require is one dollar per goat sold on the soon-to-be-established Goat Checkoff Initiative. All proceeds go to charity. Where does charity begin? At home.

I will see that it gets there. You are welcome.—*BJ*

The Legend of Tom Munn

From classic to cowboy.

My late friend Tom Munn was the son of a classically trained pianist. Tom was born in New York and how he ended up smoking dope with a gang of hippies in Aspen, Colorado, in the late fifties is a mystery.

A lusty young cowboy for the Vaugner Brothers Ranch at Woody Creek had gone to Aspen one Friday night to see if the free-love idea was actually practiced by the hippie girls or if it was only a philosophical construct purely theoretical in nature. Tom and the cowboy struck up a friendship and when the festivities were over, the cowboy suggested Tom come to the Vaugner for breakfast. Grandma Vaugner took great pride in creating and serving a traditional breakfast for the neighbors, family members, and ranch cowboys assembled to kick off the several days needed to gather Vaugner cattle out of the high country every fall.

Tom accepted the invitation, but when he got to headquarters long before daylight, he knocked on the door of the main house instead of the bunkhouse. Clyde Vaugner opened the door, looked at the bedraggled wannabe hippie standing on the front porch, and said: "By gawd! Anybody who will get up this early to come hunting a job deserves a chance. You're hired. Go down to the bunkhouse and have someone get a saddle out of the tack room and catch a horse for you, then come back up for breakfast. We are going to start the gather this morning."

Tom claims he had been horseback before, but on a beautifully carved wooden one that loped in a circle with musical accompaniment. His friend fixed him up with an old hat and a pair of worn-out chaps someone had hung on the wall in the tack room, but decided, wisely, to skip the spurs. They picked out a saddle, adjusted the stirrups to fit Tom, and saddled a twenty-year-old dog-gentle gray mare. The old mare was cow wise and kid wise. She had taught a couple of generations of Vaugner kids to ride.

Tom's friend tied the reins together so Tom would not drop them and positioned the old mare behind Clyde. He rode behind Tom so he could ride up and kick the mare in the butt when she tried to stop and graze. The old mare apparently blamed Tom for the kicks in her rear and managed to rub him out of the saddle on several handy tree limbs.

Clyde would look back, laugh, and say, "Hang in there, old kid, we'll make a cowboy out of you before dark." Tom worked for Vaugner Brothers Ranch for over twenty years until they retired and sold the ranch in the late seventies.

The bachelor cowboy life suited Tom like pine nuts suit a squirrel. He bought an old guitar, taught himself to play it upside down and backwards with his left hand, and learned some old cowboy songs and poems. He even wrote a few of his own and managed to get invited to one of the early cowboy poetry gatherings held during the National Western Stock Show at the Arvada Performing Arts Center just west of Denver in January.

The morning of the gathering, Tom finished helping feed cows on Woody Creek, called his dog, a black-and-tan German shepherd the size of a half-grown buffalo, threw the guitar in back of his AMC hatchback with the dog, and headed for Arvada. Tom was almost late for the session he was scheduled for because some lady in a Mercedes rear-ended him while he was stopped at a red light. There was little damage to either car since the bumpers more or less matched, but (there is no delicate way to put this) it scared the piss out of Tom's giant German shepherd and most of it went on Tom's guitar.

Tending to be a little crowd-foundered, when Tom saw so many cars in the parking lot and the fancy Arvada Performing Arts Center, his instinct was to turn around and head right back to Woody Creek. It took a lot of talking to convince him he was among friends and everything would turn out just fine to get him backstage.

The idea of having a cowboy poetry gathering during the stock show was that since ranch people would be in town from all over the country, they would come to the gathering. It turned out ranch folks were too busy washing bulls to take time for poetry. The audience was mostly curious patrons of the upscale Arvada Performing Arts Center, more used to watching Baryshnikov dance or listening to baroque cello recitals than hearing cowboy poetry.

Tom walked backstage just as Baxter Black, who was hosting the show, introduced him to the audience and welcomed him onstage. Tom had come straight from feeding cattle and was still dressed for work wearing seven-buckle overshoes, insulated coveralls—the heater did not work very good in his little car—and a plaid cap with fur earflaps so big they looked like two dead rabbits. Tom struck a chord on his upside-down-and-backward odoriferous guitar and launched into a parody he had just written of a current

The bachelor cowboy life suited Tom like pine nuts suit a squirrel. He bought an old guitar, taught himself to play it upside down and backwards with his left hand, and learned some old cowboy songs and poems. The sophisticated, discriminating, urban audience was stunned silent.

© JOHN BARDWELL

popular song. His version went, "Oh why must I be a sheepherder in love?" The sophisticated, discriminating, urban audience was stunned silent.

Baxter Black, to his credit, never raised an eyebrow or implied that Tom was not really representative of cowboy poetry at its finest. "Well, folks," Baxter said, "it ain't gonna get more real than that." His comment gave the audience permission to laugh and applaud, and they did.

Tom Munn died a few years ago, preceded in death by the dog that was his constant companion for many years. Accidental cowboy? Well, maybe. But cowboy to the core and we all miss him. Rest in peace, old friend.—*VQ*

It's a Dog's Life

On Their Backs
Crystalin Christensen from McMinnville, Oregon, daughter, Caden, and dog, Gus, enjoy a midday break during the Jordan Valley Big Loop Rodeo. © Larry Angier

Lemme Outta Here!
Another pesky dog which is just too helpful during branding is locked in the back of the gooseneck trailer to keep him out of trouble at the Busi Ranch corral in Amador County, California. © Larry Angier

The Flying Dog

A dog flips out over a July Fourth summer snowball fight at the annual gathering of Italian cowboy families at their Blue Creek Cow Camp in the Sierra Nevada. © Larry Angier

Good Dogs, Bad Dogs

Heretics and true believers.

"The philosophy of the classroom today will be the philosophy of government tomorrow."—*Attributed to Abraham Lincoln*

It was rude of me to throw cutworms in the Kool-Aid during "Water in the West: A Roundtable Discussion" on Saturday morning at the 2013 National Cowboy Poetry Gathering in Elko, Nevada. Irrigation uses nearly eighty percent of the water in western states, but there did not appear to be anyone on the panel who earns most or even any of their living using irrigation water to produce crops or livestock.

The panel members on the roundtable were, in my opinion, classic examples of what Eric Hoffer described in his book, "The True Believers." Hoffer wrote that political mass movements are not led by grassroots people but by dissatisfied intellectuals seeking fame and fortune or unhappy with the direction society is taking. It is common for a true believer to conclude that ordinary people left to make their own decisions will end up doing all the wrong things. It is also common for true believers to conclude they are better equipped through superior educations and greater intelligence to direct and regulate the lives of ordinary people. They create dogma and invent attractive slogans to achieve notoriety or advance their agendas. There is an alarming tendency to adopt junk science in support of their arguments. A myopic faith in the pronouncements of charismatic leaders causes those who question the ideas or oppose their leaders to be labeled bad dogs and heretics.

A brief study of history shows what happens to bad dogs and heretics. True believers instigate a good deal of the social progress that we ordinary folk should be grateful for; however, they have also led us into numerous disasters. We grassroots folk, who lack a true-believer gene and prefer to tend our own grass and leave our neighbor free to tend his, risk our own freedom. We need to be aware of how public-policy changes are often based on faith rather than fact and are advanced by self-aggrandizing intellectuals.

Our family's history of using and losing water in the West to produce crops and livestock for over a century provides a living example of how individuals like those on the roundtable have always made a significant impact on family fortunes. If we serve their agenda as good dogs, we prosper. If we are seen as bad dogs obstructing their agenda, we risk being regulated out of business.

My great-grandfather, J.P. Quinlan, came through Ellis Island in 1873 from Ireland and used the mining law to file on several famous copper and silver claims in Pitkin, Lake, and Routt counties in Colorado. In 1887, he located his family where Rock Creek joins the Grand River and filed a homestead there in 1899. The Grand River was renamed the Colorado River in 1921. JP prospered as a good dog, supported and subsidized because his activities served political and economic agendas he may or may not have understood.

A small band of Ute Indians led by a man named Yarmonite had wintered for many years on the land where JP homesteaded. As a result of the Meeker Massacre in 1879, Utes were banished

It is common for a true believer to conclude that ordinary people left to make their own decisions will end up doing all the wrong things. It is also common for true believers to conclude they are better equipped through superior educations and greater intelligence to direct and regulate the lives of ordinary people. There is an alarming tendency to adopt junk science in support of their arguments.

The Hound of the Believers

Sir Brodie at three months. A good dog and a true believer in food producers, but not in self-aggrandizing intellectuals. © *C.J. Hadley*

from all but a small area in southwestern Colorado. A small number of renegade Utes continued to winter on the spot until JP arrived and claimed the land. Yarmonite and his tiny band were deemed bad dogs and deprived of what we see today as basic rights because they were in the way of a political and economic agenda promoted by true believers as Manifest Destiny.

The agenda supported by members of the roundtable became apparent as the discussion progressed. Cities were lauded for their progressive efforts to reduce their carbon footprint and regulate water use. Today's young people were said to prefer living in cities to limit their individual carbon footprint and reduce global warming. It was repeatedly pointed out that twenty percent of the population in the West uses eighty percent of the water. Fish, wildlife, myriad endangered species, and enlightened city dwellers are denied their fair share by archaic western water laws favoring farmers and ranchers.

The twenty percent can either delay the inevitable by financing courtroom water wars that pit farmers and ranchers against other stakeholders and leave farmer-owned ditch companies crippled and broke or change our livestock operations to use little or no irrigation water. Imagine the West as one giant steer pasture. Western agriculture may be allowed to use water to produce high-value vegetable, fruit, and nut crops for human consumption, but it will not be allowed forever to use water flows with a market value of thousands of dollars to produce forage crops for animal feed that are worth only a fraction of the water's value.

The first proposal to move water from the Colorado's western slope to Denver was made in 1882. Water from rural eastern Nevada is under assault and could eventually flow south to the urban eighty percent when that water is needed in Vegas to provide growth and jobs. The water roundtable offered specious solutions to the problem by suggesting that stakeholders need only compromise and work together to achieve "win-win" outcomes for everyone concerned. In today's world, Yarmonite would be advised to accept the illusion of win-win, build a campfire, and sing folk songs with my grandfather and the U.S. Army. Yarmonite and his people would lose their winter camp in a kinder and more musical way.

In 1970, our family decided to try our hand at raising alfalfa and livestock at nearly eight thousand feet in the San Luis Valley of Colorado. The only month we could depend on being totally frost free was July. I shortly started reading about the coming ice age and predictions of disaster from the National Academy of Sciences, NASA, and the CIA predicting massive global cooling that would result in instability worldwide.

During the first Earth Day in 1970, environmentalists like Neil Calder and experts like Kenneth E.F. Watt contributed to the alleged scientific consensus with absurd statements like Calder's, "The threat of a new ice age must now stand alongside nuclear war as a likely source of wholesale death and misery for mankind." And Watt, on air pollution and global cooling: "If present trends continue, the world will be about four degrees colder for the global mean temperature in 1990, but eleven degrees colder by the year 2000.... This is about twice what it would take to put us in an ice age."

I was also reading silly essays like "Overpopulation and the Potential for Ecocide," by Paul Erlich ("The Population Bomb") and Dr. John Holdren (President Obama's science czar), warning that human activities like farming, urbanization, deforestation, and burning fossil fuel would cause an ice age that might be followed by global warming.

All this scared the hell out of me. I had just bet what few resources my family had on a plan to earn a living from agriculture at a high elevation in Colorado. According to the experts, we were doomed. I would probably lose my only frost-free month to the coming ice age. My crops would fail, my livestock would starve during the long winters, and my family would become destitute long before the anticipated global warming could save us. The exact opposite of what the experts were predicting actually happened.

The same true believers who were predicting disaster for my family from an impending ice age are now beating the drum for a global-warming disaster and demanding that they be granted the political power to regulate our activities and protect us from ourselves. I do not know if global warming is man caused. I do not know if reducing greenhouse gases will prevent further warming. But I do know we grassroots folk should carefully consider actual facts and not be frightened into granting political power to true believers like the ones riding the ice-age horse to fame and fortune in the 1970s.

Several of these same scientists have switched to the global-warming horse today. These true believers, like the panel members on the Water in the West roundtable discussion in Elko, have books to sell, papers to write, lecture fees to collect, reputations to develop, a living to earn, and other agendas that we common folk may or may not understand.—*VQ*

Try Me!
There is a pause in the action as Fish and Ricky try to get a trotty pair to the corral from the late spring pasture. There's one in every crowd, but Fish isn't backing down! © Alyssa Wilcox

Working Kids

Looping the Kid
"Grandpa, let me go!"
Stan Dell'Orto ropes his oldest grandson, Waylon, at the Wooster
family calf branding in Copperopolis, California. © Robin Dell'Orto

Checking the Cows

"I can count!"
One-year-old Maezy Rae
Smith checks cows with her
father, Spencer Smith, who is
a cowboy at the DS Ranch
in Sierra Valley, California.
© Abbey Smith

Leo & Leatherwood's Wedding

A lack of fashion sense in upscale Texas.

How Leo Gardunio and Jimmy Leatherwood became such good friends might seem odd to some folks. Jimmy was from a prominent Texas family involved in banking, insurance and assorted other businesses in a part of Texas where a significant number of citizens were still mad at Santa Anna. Leo had probably never been over a hundred miles from the San Luis Valley of Colorado where his people settled on a huge tract of land granted to Carlos Beaubien and Narcissus Lee by Mexico's Governor Manuel Armijo long before the Southwest became part of the United States.

Jimmy had decided to help pay his way through college with a semi hauling alfalfa from our place to dairy farms in Texas. Jimmy would leave after his last class on Friday, show up to load on Saturday, and be back for Tuesday morning classes.

The joking and teasing banter that developed between Jimmy and Leo made the heavy bales seem lighter and the loading go faster than normal. Jimmy called Leo his favorite wetback. Leo denied being a wetback and claimed his people were here minding their own business before gringos like Jimmy invaded and started fighting over who owned the land they had stolen from the right-

Jimmy called Leo his favorite wetback. Leo denied being a wetback and claimed his people were here minding their own business before gringos like Jimmy invaded and started fighting over who owned the land they had stolen from the rightful owners.

ful owners. Leo also insisted he had never left Mexico. Mexico had left him and he was a legally adopted U.S. citizen through the Treaty of Guadalupe Hidalgo.

Leo knew one of his great-grandmothers was an Indian from the Taos Pueblo and when he found a menorah in his basement that had belonged to his other great-grandmother, I told him what I thought it was. A professor in Santa Fe, New Mexico, told Leo all about it and explained how Sephardic Jews were forced to convert to Catholicism and take Spanish names or be expelled from Spain. Many of them continued to practice Judaism in secret. Some signed on to leave for America at the first opportunity.

When Jimmy told us he was to be married upon graduation from college, Leo claimed there was no way a rich Texan could invite a poor Mexican to his wedding, but jokingly asked about inviting a poor Indian Jew half-breed.

Jimmy never said a word to Leo, but took me aside and made me promise to bring Leo to the wedding. Leo was thrilled when he received the elegant engraved invitation.

Leo, unaware of the current fashion of narrow lapels and skin-

© JOHN BARDWELL

**Leo asked me how he looked.
I did not have the heart to tell him
he looked for all the world like
a Mexican Mafia hit man.**

ny ties, took his twenty-year-old suit with lapels wide enough to land a plane on to the cleaners and had my wife select a too-wide tie from his collection of three. Leo's antique suit, still in the plastic wrapper from the cleaners, was carefully hung in the motel closet. He had apparently washed his definitely not-permanent-pressed white shirt himself. To say it was wrinkled would be a gross understatement. It looked like an albino prune. Fortunately, there was an ironing board and iron available. Unfortunately, I lacked certain domestic skills. Fortunately, the scorch marks were mostly on the back and as long as Leo kept his suit coat on nobody would notice.

It turned out that I was more familiar with diamond hitches than Windsor knots, but after several tries a more or less acceptable result was achieved. Leo was built like a fireplug and his suit sort of fit, kind of. Bathed and shaved, hair slicked down, and smelling of Aqua Velva, Leo was nervous but ready to meet the elite citizens of Erath County, Texas. He asked me how he looked. I did not have the heart to tell him he looked for all the world like a Mexican Mafia hit man.

When he looked up at the reception and saw Leo grinning at him with all three carefully brushed teeth, Jimmy came across the room, took Leo by the elbow, and made a circle introducing Leo to every guest, saying, "This is my friend Leo from Colorado."

I leaned up against the wall and thought about the many reasons I had always liked Jimmy Leatherwood.—*VQ*

Geezerhood Blues

If you have a degree in Elizabethan literature, it isn't my fault.

You know that 1973 Ford pickup you have been keeping around for the last five decades? Just like those of us firmly in the grips of geezerhood, the old truck is plumb worn-out and ready to be towed to the junkyard. The transmission is slipping, it bleeds oil, the entire exhaust system needs replacing. The floorboards are rusting out along with the tailgate. It is hard to start and needs yet another new battery. If you are a geezer, perhaps you can identify and sympathize with these disturbing symptoms of age and misuse. Your vintage pickup is headed to the salvage yard. You, my fellow or future geezer, are headed to the marble orchard. (Get over it. Just like your old truck, you had a long and pretty good run...)

Along the way, you have learned a lot. Most of it the hard way. Experience is the best teacher, but it is also pretty darn expensive. As the yuppies of yore used to say (and as a generous public service), I will "share" with the reading public some pearls of geezer wisdom.

You are *not* entitled to the money someone else has earned, ever. This concept is out of favor these days, but that doesn't make it any less true. This has nothing to do with charity or anyone voluntarily giving money away. As a certified geezer, I prefer choosing my own ways to waste my relatively insignificant amounts of cash.

If man buns ever become a fashion requirement, I will consider changing genders. This may require some research because now there are apparently more than two genders to choose from.

Never argue with anyone about politics, religion or the color of a horse. Everyone already has his/her mind made up. Not only are you wasting your breath, there is also a good possibility you will alienate a potential friend. And you certainly don't need any more enemies. This is not a small issue. Especially the horse-color thing.

Political correctness is the worst thing that has happened to this country since line dancing and nonalcoholic beer. Most often it is an obvious attempt to stifle free speech. But, as a geezer, you are given some freedom to pretty much say whatever you like. Folks who find it offensive can write it off as "dementia." You are old. Geezers are cut some slack.

Any grown man who wears a "man bun" should lose points on the masculinity scale. It makes them look like Ruth Buzzi on the old "Laugh-In" television show. If man buns ever become a fashion requirement, I will consider changing genders. This may require some research because now there are apparently more than two genders to choose from.

If you have a college degree in something like Elizabethan literature, have $75,000 in student-loan debt and still can't find a job, it is not the fault of us geezers. You should have taken a welding course. Do you know how unmarketable (totally useless), for

example, a four-year college degree is in a subject like, say, psychology? Well, I've got one. I rest my case.

At the Cracker Barrel we geezers know all about those items hanging on the walls. It is the same stuff we have back at our houses. Nevertheless, it is somewhat disconcerting to have photos of someone's long-dead grandmother watching you scarf down your chicken fried steak. Don't be too alarmed—you may end up there yourself someday.

Getting back to the old-pickup-truck theme, another geezer analogy may be appropriate here. A few months back my geezer fuel pump (translation: heart) needed a major overhaul. My bride of nearly half a century was with me the night before surgery.

"Bill," she says glumly, "there is something I have to talk to you about..."

What could this possibly be about? Some dark secret from the distant past? Or perhaps some tearful and emotional speech about what a great husband I have been? Charming. Witty. Fantastic lover. (On reflection, I quickly nixed that possibility.)

Anyway, this is what she said, and I am *not* making this up.

"I have been thinking. If you die...well, who is going to do our taxes?"—*BJ*

The Aspen Hut

When the new outhouse was built at the Dufurrena Ranch summer sheep and cow camp, the new lumber was a total eyesore in this grove of Nevada aspens so Carolyn Dufurrena painted it camo. © *Carolyn Fox*

"You Can't Make This Stuff up!"

Crackin' Up

Leland and Regina Schneider and their pups at Brown Cow Camp in Tulare County, California.
© Larry Angier

Secrets

Waylon Dell'Orto and cousin
Elsie Brooks play in the hay
barn at the Levaggi Ranch in
Plymouth, California.
© Robin Dell'Orto

Of Mice and Women

Charles Darwin would be proud.

For the last twenty-five years a war has been fought at the family farm. The enemy? Mice. The battles have been brutal and savage, but recent developments indicate that perhaps the war has escalated to a new level. The mice are winning.

This new generation of rodents is infinitely smarter than the ones from previous years. The sneaky little bastards have learned to remove bait from mousetraps without paying the fatal consequences. Like starving Ethiopians, they devour anything that even looks like food. With all the dumb mice having succumbed to the executioner's spring trap, only the best and brightest mice remain. Survival of the fittest. Evolution and natural selection in action. Charles Darwin would be proud.

Hope arrives in the form of a "mouse glue trap." A little peanut butter as bait and, like a fat guy at an all-you-can-eat dessert bar, the mice have no willpower or defense. It is D-day for this race of Super Mice. It is the beginning of the end for the evil and hated Mice Reich. But as with all battle strategies, there is a small glitch. Or, maybe, a big glitch. Only time will tell.

One morning last week my bride of forty years informed me she had caught another mouse in her kitchen cupboard. "I will

Halfway through I realize that maybe it is not a good idea to introduce the concept that old, fat, essentially useless males should be unceremoniously sent to the slaughterhouse.

take care of him," I reply, gloating over another successful skirmish. (What do I mean by "take care of him"? Think Tony Soprano here.)

"Don't bother," wife says. "I turned him loose."

What? This is the first step to an unconditional surrender. Giving aid and comfort to the enemy. Treason.

"He looked so pitiful," spouse continues. "His little legs were going ninety miles an hour. At least the two that were not stuck in the super glue."

This, mind you, from the same woman who has no qualms about removing decapitated mice from regular mousetraps. Plus, I have been subject to homicidal rants recently directed at innocent little squirrels invading her backyard bird feeder.

"How did you release him?" I ask, knowing the mousetrap glue is the stickiest substance known to man.

"Well," she says, still unrepentant. "We can just say it wasn't easy. In fact, it was an unpleasant experience for all concerned."

A little education is perhaps in order here. I explain to her, like the patient and long-suffering husband I am, that during World War II folks were routinely shot for similar incidents. I also make comparisons to Jane Fonda, Benedict Arnold, and that guy in Iraq

© JOHN BARDWELL

who abandoned his post. (This last thing was maybe a little too much, but what the heck. I was on a roll.)

Perhaps I should have realized my lovely bride has some soft spots in her psyche. For example, we quit raising beef for home consumption as she made pets of the steers on death row. She hand-fed them doughnuts. They followed her around the farm like puppies. A trip to the meat packer on execution day was like a somber trek to the funeral home. Never name, by the way, any animal you intend to eat.

A few weeks back I mentioned that I was "shipping" one of our herd bulls. "Where are you shipping him?" she innocently inquires.

"McDonalds," I say, and instantly regret it.

"You mean that nice big black one across the road?" she asks, alarmed.

I then explain my decision by noting this bull is simply too old, too fat, and has absolutely no interest in doing his assigned duties. Halfway through I realize that maybe it is not a good idea to introduce the concept that old, fat, essentially useless males should be unceremoniously sent to the slaughterhouse. I quickly change the subject.

But I digress. Back to the spouse and the mouse. Wife is vainly trying to justify her mouse-releasing offense.

"I don't think we will have any trouble from this particular mouse," she offers, "as his mobility is severely compromised. All that glue and everything. In fact, I think he will probably be put on the disability list." (I know you think I am making this up. I assure you these are her exact words.)

The severely traumatized and glue-wounded mouse never surfaces again. Can't say I blame him. Hopefully he returns to the mice barracks and spreads a warning about the new glue weapon. I imagine him relating this episode to his mice buddies:

"You will never believe what just happened to me."—*BJ*

Fighting With a Gobbler

Learning about my past at a truck stop in New Mexico.

When we finally got a place of our own in partnership with a kind and generous man who was long on optimism and short on common sense, it was in a pretty bad neighborhood for agriculture. Our version of "the American dream" was in southern Colorado, nearly eight thousand feet in elevation, and blessed with only six to eight inches of moisture a year. An even more optimistic group from Holland called Freehold Land and Immigration Company built a giant reservoir based on a decimal-point error by a British engineer back in 1919, so there was only enough irrigation water for about one-tenth of the land it planned to develop, but it gave our little community an on-again, off-again supply of irrigation water.

One thing we could do as good or better than most was grow more high-quality alfalfa than needed to winter our cattle and sheep. I found some dairymen in Texas willing to pay enough for the alfalfa that we could afford to haul it to them. I bought an old cab-over Peterbilt and a set of well-used twenty-seven-foot double flatbed trailers from Forester Trucks in Amarillo and set about creating a winter job for myself hauling hay to Texas.

We'd load 620 bales on the two trailers. I'd leave after supper Sunday and drive all night so we could unload in daylight Tuesday. Over La Veta Pass then down Interstate 25 and over Raton Pass into New Mexico, then across the corner of New Mexico to Clayton. There was a New Mexico Port of Entry on top of Raton Pass and another at Clayton.

When I hauled the first load through New Mexico, the officer at Raton explained how I had to pay cash to cover the estimated fuel tax on every trip. He told me to keep the receipt to show the officer at Clayton or he would make me pay it again. I walked in the little port at Clayton and handed my paperwork to a weather-beaten old fellow sitting on a stool behind the counter. He looked at the paperwork, then asked, "Is your uncle Dddell Aldred?"

I walked in the little port at Clayton and handed my paperwork to a weather-beaten old fellow sitting on a stool behind the counter. He looked at the paperwork, then asked, "Is your uncle Dddell Aldred?"

Uh-oh, I thought. "Yes, sir, he is."

"I tttthought so. There can't be two ppeople on one planet with a name like yours. Do you remmmember spending summer with Ddell and Helen on the Red Top Ranch east of Wwwalsenburg when you were little?"

"I sure do."

"I was on that rrranch with Dell that summmmer. Do you rrremmmmenber me? I'm Stuttering Bill."

"It has been over thirty years. I would not have known you, but I remember the Stuttering Bill stories. Like the time that big albino colt went snow-blind, walked off a cutbank in a snowstorm, and broke several of Dell's ribs. You went to visit and kept making him

Angry Gobbler

Anyone who has grown up on a farm would agree that this could be a good representation of what an irate male turkey would look like just before "flogging the snot" out of a young man. One day Stuttering Bill heard a bunch of screaming and yelling: "Ttthat turkey had knocked you down. Dust was fogging, feathers were flying, and he was flogging the dddaylights out of you." © Alan Hart

Helen handed you the hatchet. You looked at that bird, then looked up at me and shook your head. You wouldn't do it. You handed the hatchet to Helen, told her to kill him, and covered up your eyes with both hands.

laugh, but it hurt so bad to laugh he called the nurse and had you thrown out of the hospital."

"I told Dell tttthat big albino colt would never amount to nothing. He was so clumsy he'd fall down walking. I told him ppppainting big black circles around that horse's eyes with shoe polish wouldn't keep him from going snow-blind either. That hhhorse was just plain dumb and big black circles around those ugly red eyes mmmade him look even dumber. He was the wwworst horse I ever saw."

"Sammy Grimsley told me about the time you and Dell were in Sammy's Wonder Bar in Walsenburg. Some fellow got loud and was using bad language in front of the lady tending bar. Dell asked her to get him some coffee and when she brought it, Dell grabbed the guy and tried to pour that hot coffee in his shirt pocket. You went to court as a character witness and told the judge he should go easy since Dell was only trying to defend the lady's honor. The judge said: 'Hell, I have known that woman for thirty years. She ain't got no honor left to defend.' He fined Dell a hundred dollars for starting a fight and disturbing the peace."

"Do you remember ttthat turkey?"

"You bet! I fought that damn turkey all summer."

"Helen had quite a bbbunch of tturkeys. Most of them were pretty nice turkeys, bbut a young gobbler got your number. One day I heard a bunch of screaming and yelling. Ttthat turkey had knocked

Uncle Dell's wife, Aunt Helen, at the Gypsum Canyon Ranch in Colorado. She was scared of nothing.

94

you down. Dust was fogging, feathers were flying, and he was flogging the daylights out of you. I rrran out, kicked him off, and carried you to the bbbarn. You weren't hurt but you were mad as hell. After that, whenever you would try to run to the barn, that turkey wwwould chase you back to the house. Helen had an old dust mop and had me cut the handle shorter so you cccould handle it good and told you the turkey would be afraid of the dust mop. She said if you shook it at him, he'd leave you alone.

"The next evening when we were putting the horses up, I heard a fight start. That ttturkey was not the least bit afraid of the dust mmop. He was flogging the hell out of it. You were poking at him with the dust mop, bbacking toward the barn one step at a time, and cussing that turkey every step. You sure knew a lot of bbad words for such a little bboy. I said, 'Well, I better go rescue him.' Dell said: 'Nnno, I'd kind of like to see how long this can go on. He mmight figure out how to kill that turkey with the dust mop.'

Wild Turkey Contest

These gobblers exhibit unusual behaviors in their attempts to establish dominance. Opportunities to see open confrontations between two equally matched males are extremely rare in the wild. © *Alan Hart*

"Your birthday came on Thanksgiving day that year. Helen said we would have a birthday pppparty for you. You were gonna be five. She said you could get even with that ttturkey because we would have him for Thanksgiving dddinner and you could chop his head off.

"The day before Thanksgiving, Helen wanted to get the bird ready. We caught him, Dell tied his wings, and laid him on the chopping block. I grabbed his head and stretched his neck out. Helen handed you the hatchet. You looked at that bird, then looked up at me and shook your head. You wouldn't do it. You handed the hatchet to Helen, told her to kill him, and covered up your eyes with both hands. I saw you flinch when Helen chopped off his head.

"There were a lot of cowboys there for your birthday. That turkey sure tasted good for such an ornery bird. We ate every bit of him."—*VQ*

Ranching, Blasphemy & Other Unpardonable Sins

Without sin, politics, at least as we know it, would cease to exist.

A couple of Sundays ago our minister at church gave a sermon on sin. As the old joke goes, he is definitely "agin it." I learned a lot more about sin than I really wanted to know. First, there are two kinds of sin. Sins of *commission* are things you knew were wrong but did them anyway. That pretty much covers most of them—at least in my case. Then there are sins of *omission*, which are things you should have done but, for whatever reason, failed to do. Any retribution for these sins I hope is a little less serious than the first kind. It is akin to getting a hangover when you never even took a drink.

Anyway, it got me thinking about sin. A lot of things that used to be sins aren't sins anymore. Gambling, for example, used to be a sin but now is promoted by a whole bunch of state governments in the form of the lottery. It used to be known as the "numbers racket" and was administered by

"God Judging Adam," 1795, by William Blake (1757-1827).

our Italian friends. Now you can buy a lottery ticket in almost any convenience store in the country. My old friend Frank, a good Catholic, used to sneak to eat steak on Friday when it was considered wrong to eat anything but fish. Frank has since passed away and I worry that he may now be shoveling coal in some very unpleasant place—like Rock Springs, Wyoming—simply as a consequence of doing something that ain't even a sin anymore.

What if all sins were eliminated overnight? First off, a lot of televangelists would have to get real jobs. Jesus, I learned in Sunday school, did not live in an eighteen-million-dollar mansion and travel around in a Lear jet. Mostly he crashed at other folks' houses and his transportation was the Sandal Leather Express. However, there is one documented case that a donkey was briefly employed. (At this point I will refrain from making any televangelist/donkey comparison jokes...although it is difficult.) But there is some very credible evidence that Jesus' companions drove Japanese vehicles: "The disciples were all in one Accord."

A society without sin would have a profound effect on the ranching/farming community. Right off the bat, a lot of auctioneers at the sale barn would have to quit taking bids from those invisible guys in the back row. Order buyers would quit meeting for coffee before the sale and winking at one another during the bidding. Feedlot buyers now would explain how a truckload of cattle can "shrink" after traveling just a few miles down the road. Somebody (who, I don't have a clue) could truthfully explain how no matter how low cattle prices go, the meat prices in grocery stores stay the same. These, and other age-old mysteries, would be immediately solved.

> **I don't know about you, but I did not work my way to the top of the food chain to subsist on tofu and black beans—although black beans are extremely edible if you toss in a ham hock during the cooking process.**

A lot of animal rights' activists consider all animal agriculture to be wrong. Sinful even. If they are correct, that is the end of most ranches and farms. I don't know about you, but I did not work my way to the top of the food chain to subsist on tofu and black beans—although black beans are extremely edible if you toss in a ham hock during the cooking process. Elimination of animal agriculture would mean no more bacon, hamburgers, lamb chops, turkey, ham, McNuggets, eggs, hot dogs, milk, cheese and, God help us all, ice cream. If these extremists have their way it is just the beginning of the slippery slope that will result in giving chickens the right to vote.

Without sin, a whole lot of people will be standing in the unemployment line. Politics, at least as we know it, would cease to exist. Policemen, judges, jailers, probation officers, lawyers, brand inspectors, and anyone connected to our judicial system would not be needed. The same goes for horse traders, dope dealers, Amway salesmen, ditch riders, and locksmiths. Out of business. I am confident you can think of a lot more based on your personal experiences. Even my old friend Paul, who is retired and doesn't work a lick, would have to give up on fishing. Fishing and lying kind of go hand in hand. A guy might as well pack it in if he can't lie about catching fish.

So you see, a world without sin would not be all that it is cracked up to be. Our economy, bad enough already, would come to a grinding halt. Our world would change so much we might not even recognize the place anymore. There is only one thing you can do to save western civilization. And you folks know what that is, don't you?—*BJ*

Grandpas, Fathers & Sons

Simply tradition.

Overseeing the Branding

Young cowboy Rance Hannah, son of Zack and Amy Hannah, oversees the Alturas Ranches' calf branding in Likely, California. © Kathy DeForest

Watching or Helping?
Duke Vance and son, Alden, help at spring branding
on Howard Mesa Cattle Company north of Williams, Arizona.
© Kathy McCraine

My Grandpas Are the Best
Knox Wyatt Dell'Orto has his stirrups adjusted by
his grandfathers, Steve Wooster and Stan Dell'Orto,
on his first early morning gather.
© Robin Dell'Orto

Busted!

"Dammit, Bill, why did you let me see you?"

It was just before midnight when I pulled across the scale at Clayton, New Mexico. Stuttering Bill was on duty and flashed the lights telling me to come into the office. Bill knew all my mother's brothers and worked on ranches with them before signing on to work the late shift at the New Mexico Port of Entry to support his little bunch of cows.

The port scale at Raton said the loaded truck weighed just over 78,000 pounds, so it was well under the 80,000-pound gross limit. The thirteen-year-old Cabover Peterbilt was built in 1962 and nearly wore out hauling milk for Texas dairymen, and the well-used twenty-seven-foot-long set of doubles I had bought from the Forester truck dealership in Amarillo weighed a little over 34,000 pounds. The 620 bales of bright green alfalfa we loaded that morning weighed a near-perfect average of seventy-one pounds.

Bill did not stutter much anymore, except when he was upset or angry. He was named Stuttering Bill by one of the four-year-old twin girls of the rancher who sort of unofficially adopted him because she had a friend named Bill who giggled in church. She called one Giggling Bill and the other Stuttering Bill so everyone would know which Bill she was talking about. The name stuck even though Bill had mostly outgrown the affliction.

"Wwwell, son, that's a damn fine-looking load of alfalfa. Those

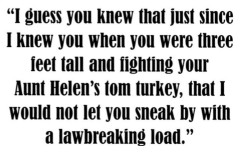

"I guess you knew that just since I knew you when you were three feet tall and fighting your Aunt Helen's tom turkey, that I would not let you sneak by with a lawbreaking load."

dairy cows in Texas will be glad to see that. Your outfit finally learned how to load hay straight on those trailers. Some of the first ones you came through here with were pretty scary, bulging out on both sides. I almost made you unload and reload a couple of times. I guess you knew that just since I knew you when you were three feet tall and fighting your Aunt Helen's tom turkey, that I would not let you sneak by with a lawbreaking load. If you hadn't had about fourteen ropes and six extra cable come-alongs tying those bales on, I would have made you reload."

There would be no favoritism as long as Bill was drawing wages from the state of New Mexico. He would represent the state and do his job as best he could. Except for one thing. When it was slow there was a good chance of being treated to a Stuttering Bill story, and this was one of those special nights.

"My trying to decide to make you reload or not caused me to think about the time my best friend arrested me and impounded my pack mules.

"You know how The Dddust Bbbowl and Ddddepression killed my daddy and caused my mother to marry a liar and a thief hoping to keep her family together? How my stepfather headed to California with his new family and ran out of gas for his old truck and running short of food abandoned me? Charlie found me sitting on a rock staring at a burned-out campfire when he followed the trail back where my stepfather had siphoned five gallons of gas out of Charlie's old cattle truck. I guess I was sitting on the llluckiest rock in Colorado because I ended up with as good a family as the Dust Bowl had cost me.

"Charlie not only sent me to school with the twins, he insisted I take part in every activity. I don't think the family ever missed a single basketball game. I wasn't all that good at school, but I was a fair basketball player. I would drive the ranch pickup to school when we had basketball practice and would be too late for the bus home. Charlie and the twins would milk and do my chores on those nights, but insisted I never miss a practice.

"Our senior year, there were only three of us—Cecil, Bob and me—in a class with three boys and four girls, but there were three big stout town kids in the junior class, and we went to the state championships in Fort Collins. We got beat in the third round by some little town in Weld County, but we had a lot of fun.

"The three of us were best friends all through high school and still are. Cecil's dad had an insurance office in town. Cecil took over the business when his dad retired and became justice of the peace. Bob went on to college and became a game warden for the state of Colorado. Charlie tried to get me to go to college with Bob, but I loved the ranch and Charlie was getting older so I wanted to stay and learn all the things he could teach me. I figured the things Charlie had taught me and would continue to teach me would beat a college education any day.

"Early one warm morning in June, after we had moved the cows up on the forest, I loaded the mules, Millie and Mollie, with all the salt and mineral blocks they would agree to carry, put four new meat sacks in the panniers, saddled old Jigaboo and headed for the high country.

"Elk, like cows, love the salt and mineral blocks. I tied Jigaboo and the mules in the tttimber and slipped back down the ridge where I would have a clear shot. I did not have to wait too long for

A family reunion at Dell's place in Gypsum Canyon, Colorado, in the thirties. Opposite: *Vess, fifteen months.*

them to come. I picked out a nice fat spike. By the time I got him quartered up, sacked up, and in the panniers it was afternoon. I'd get home about dddark.

"Most of us lived on wild meat. It took most of the calves we raised to keep the bank paid, but killing the state's elk in June was damn sure illegal. On the steepest part of the trail there is a giant rock that bbblocks the view up or down the trail. Just at the point where the trail switched back around the rock, who should I meet but my friend Bob.

"Bob folded his hands on the saddle horn and frowned. 'What's in the panniers, spike or dry cow?'

"'Spike.'

"'I expect you did a nice job and it is in clean meat sacks.'

"'Yep.'

"'The cooks at the school will be glad of that. Remember all the elk and deer burgers we ate when we were in school?'

"'Yep.'

"'You know I have to write you a summons, take your mules and deliver the meat, then Cecil is going to have to fine you for killing elk out of season?'

"'Yep.'

"'This is a lot of work. You have ruined my whole day. Dammit, Bill, why did you let me see you?'

"You know," Stuttering Bill said to me, "if it had not been for all those ropes and the six extra cable cccome-alongs holding those sloppy looking loads on those trailers, I would have made you rrrreload them."

Yep.—*VQ*

101

Slouching Toward Geezerhood

To me, a Smart Phone is a Chinese puzzle.

© JOHN BARDWELL

If you are fortunate to live long enough before taking that inevitable "dirt nap" that awaits us all, there are two unavoidable consequences: (1) You *will* grow old—with all the unpleasant symptoms associated with the process. (2) You won't like it. (Not only will you not like it, you will also notice some interesting phenomena that will occur despite anything you do to prevent/delay them.) As a public service I will graciously attempt to warn you of some of these things as you slouch, shuffle and limp toward official geezer status. If you are already a geezer, you can make up your own list.

Almost everything will irritate you. Recently at the cattle sale barn, the little café was out of coconut *crème* pie. This was extremely distressing since it is the *only* reason I go there in the first place. I make a mental note to go an hour early next week to keep some miserable SOB from eating all the pie.

I keep three horses for no apparent reason. (Actually, two-and-a-half horses.

Two quarter horses and a pony.) They have not been ridden in fifteen years. They stand around, eat, look for hand-outs, and, since they are geldings, have no interest in reproductive activities. Does this make any sense? This is also irritating—especially once the realization occurs that your horses share the same characteristics as you....

Technology is advancing so fast that, as a full-fledged geezer, you can't keep up. Not only that, you don't want to. Just last month I learned to stop that flashing light on my VCR. (By the way, VCRs went out a decade ago.) A Smart Phone is a Chinese puzzle. My granddaughter, age eight, helps me with mine. Just the other day I asked her for some help. (I ain't, by the way, making this up.)

"Grandpa," she says, "I already showed you this twice. Next time you are on your own." If she wasn't so unbelievably adorable and smart, I would find this irritating too.

As an official geezer, you will make

The definition of middle age is when you are home alone on a Saturday night and the phone rings and you pray it is not for you.

unwise financial decisions. After raising cattle for thirty years I can count on one hand the times I made any money. Why do you do it? Well, first it is hard to describe yourself as a cattle farmer/rancher if you don't own any cows. Plus, I like seeing the new calves in the spring and eating pie at the sale barn. It is beginning to be an expensive hobby.

Watching television is irritating. I have over a hundred channels and can't find anything to watch. The morning news shows are especially revolting. All that giggling and "happy talk," even by those short-skirt-wearing beauty queens, is so contrived it becomes nauseating. Nobody is that happy. I usually end up watching the nature channels, as animals do not have any hidden political agendas. My favorite shows involve some mental midget handling poisonous snakes.

Another thing about these television news people. After any major tragedy/catastrophe the cameras show up and some "journalist" sticks a microphone in some grieving victims' faces. If they are overcome with emotion and weeping, that is especially newsworthy. This is more than irritating. It is pathetic, inexcusable and a shameless ploy for ratings. I feel like slapping somebody.

Someone said once that the definition of middle age is when you are home alone on a Saturday night and the phone rings and you pray it is not for you. I am not pushing middle age. I have been dragging it for years. As a geezer, you are on your own timetable. For example, the other night me and my bride of many

decades were in bed at almost nine o'clock. The phone rings. "Who," she says, "could possibly be calling us this late?" My response is not to answer it. Whoever is calling...well, I do not want to talk to them. "Maybe you should answer. Could be somebody died."

I recall that this same thing happened to Rodney, my rancher friend from North Dakota. I used his line: "Somebody died? Well, they will still be dead in the morning."

There are a few surprises as you stumble your way through geezerhood. I am on Facebook (primarily to see pictures of my granddaughters), and the last few months I have been getting "friend requests" from some very attractive young women I don't know. Coincidentally they are all showing a little "cleavage." I simply can't figure out why they want to be friends with a seventy-year-old "has been" with bad knees and hip, heart problems and diabetes. A great mystery, but flattering nonetheless.

Since my bride also has access to my Facebook page, I thought it would be wise to ask permission to "friend" these young partially clothed beauties. Her short answer includes a suggestion I do something disgusting and physically impossible with my laptop. The sad part of this incident is...well, I was kind of relieved. I already have all the friends I need and can afford.

One more thing. As a responsible geezer it is important that you practice and learn these words: "Get off my lawn!"—*BJ*

Comfort

Freshly unloaded from a truck, these beautiful Belgian mares huddle together in the corral. Almost overnight their lives have been turned upside down because their owner has died. These lifetime companions stand patiently, drawing comfort from each other. They don't know it, but, lucky for them, they have just arrived in the "last best place"—Montana. © Cynthia Baldauf

The Ginger Belgians

Mr. McPherson's advice.

Delfino came by today. He was one of our hired-man Leo's many uncles and my favorite. Delfino came to visit most often. This day he was on his way home from attending his old friend Mr. McPherson's funeral and wanted to talk about the old days and how he and Mr. McPherson became friends.

"You didn't know Mister McPherson," Delfino said. "He was long before your time when San Acacio, Colorado, called itself the cauliflower capital of the world. We called him Mac the Cauliflower Man among ourselves, but otherwise we called him Mister McPherson. He taught us to grow cauliflower and bought all we could grow to ship back east, on ice, in boxcars.

"I farmed the same one-hundred-and-sixty acres my son grows beer barley for Coors on with his new center pivot sprinkler. My grandfather and father farmed there before me. When Mama and I married, her father made us a wedding present of a fine pair of two-year-old ginger Belgians. I named them Solomon and Salome.

"I would grow eighty acres of garden peas when the cannery in La Jara was still canning peas and then buy little pigs to clean up after the perfect canning peas were picked. The peas and pigs put good things into the soil so I could grow eighty acres of Red McClure potatoes the next year. When the Sanchez Reservoir was eighty in 1918, the land company brought in people from all over the world to buy farms where you are farming now. One of their slogans was Pigs, Peas, Potatoes and Prosperity and it was sort of true except there was not enough water in dry years for all the land they sold so most people went broke and moved away. Did you know that the little town of Mesita, where you get your mail, was first named Hamburg to make the German immigrants who bought land feel at home?

"When Mister McPherson taught us about cauliflower, I started growing forty acres of cauliflower and forty acres of potatoes every other year after the peas and pigs. One year, the cauliflower price was good, and I grew a record crop of over five hundred sacks of potatoes per acre. It was a lot of money, so I bought a new John Deere tractor, a plow, a cultivator, a disc, and a harrow. The other eighty had forty acres of brome and orchard grass mix to pasture my horses, milk cow, and a few lambs for meat and forty acres of alfalfa and bromegrass mix for hay to feed in the winter. The salesman

> "When it was haying time, my brothers would come with their wives and my sisters would come with their husbands. I would hook Solomon and Salome to my McCormick Deering mower, then rake with my dump rake and use Solomon and Salome on the buckrake to take bunches of hay to the beaverslide my grandfather built so many years ago.

tried to talk me into buying a hay baler and a rake so I could sell my alfalfa. I did not want a noisy hay baler to chop my hay into squares. I liked the old way.

"When it was haying time, my brothers would come with their wives and my sisters would come with their husbands. I would hook Solomon and Salome to my McCormick Deering mower, then rake with my dump rake and use Solomon and Salome on the buckrake to take bunches of hay to the beaverslide my grandfather built so many years ago. My cousin, Alonzo, would bring his team of Spanish mules to pull the rack up the beaverslide and dump the hay so my brothers could use pitchforks and place the hay just right. The kids would take turns salting each layer lightly so it would stay fresh and green all winter. It was a good time with much food and Alonzo playing his guitar and singing the old *corridos* we all knew by heart.

"When Mama started cooking at the school, we sold our milk cow and stopped raising lambs for meat since she could get milk and fresh meat at Romero's store on her way home from work.

"One day Mister McPherson stopped by and said the cauliflower crop in California was in trouble and he thought cauliflower would be worth a lot of money this year. He thought I should grow more than forty acres. I said I did not think I could grow more because I did not have enough sisters.

"Every year my sisters would come when the little cauliflowers were starting to grow in the middle of the plant and tie the leaves up with string to keep the cauliflower white and protect it from the sun.

"One day Mister McPherson stopped by and said the cauliflower crop in California was in trouble and he thought cauliflower would be worth a lot of money this year. He thought I should grow more than forty acres. I said I did not think I could grow more because I did not have enough sisters."

"Mister McPherson laughed and told me the professors with the University of California at Davis had taught the cauliflower leaves to grow up like a tent and protect the little cauliflowers from the sun. We would plant the new variety this year and not need to tie the leaves with string.

"'I never thought,' I told him, 'that I would ever be growing sisterless cauliflower. But I still cannot grow more than forty acres because I need to have forty acres in potatoes for my customers in New Mexico and Texas who come every year and buy every sack I can grow.'

"'Well,' Mister McPherson said, 'you know that alfalfa is putting the same good things into the ground that the peas and pigs do. I think if you plowed up that forty acres of alfalfa it would grow a good crop of cauliflower.'

"'Oh! I can't plow up the alfalfa because I need it to feed my horses in the winter.'

"'What do you need the horses for?' Mister McPherson asked.

"'Why to cut the alfalfa,' I said, without thinking.

"I was so embarrassed at having said something so dumb that I looked away toward the mountains trying to think what to say next so Mister McPherson would not think me a fool. But I had underestimated the man, thinking him just another gringo interested only in making money.

"He was a good friend and I will miss visiting him when I go to Alamosa. When I looked back at him, he smiled and said, 'You know what, Delfino? If I had a beautiful team of ginger Belgians like yours, I would not plow up their alfalfa either.'" —*VQ*

I've Got It!
*Dorothy La Bash is a
two-year-old Arizona
cowgirl. When not
riding her horse she
practices roping a
dummy calf.
She thinks she's
ready for a live one.*
© *Cheryl Rogos*

Bilko

A schemer, scammer and talented con artist.

Bilko Opines
"Well, now you know I'm ingenious, Billy, and I've never been ingenuous."
© Kathy McCraine

Sergeant Bilko, a fifteen-year-old stout dude-string gelding at a guest ranch in Wyoming, is a schemer, scammer and talented con artist—much like his namesake on the old television series. There is no four-footed animal smarter than a dude horse that has packed around wannabe cowboys for the last ten years or so.

Bilko, more often than not, fails to report during the morning roundups and subsequently makes the AWOL list at least a couple of times a week. Since he also knows all the best hiding

If Bilko was a human "teenager," no doubt he would be declared incorrigible in any court of law. The outfit's wranglers, a somewhat cynical bunch, all want to send Bilko on an expense-paid tour of France—in a can.

places he is often successful in taking several new "recruits" along with him. Adept at opening any and all gates, he occasionally takes a few days off to visit his horse buddies residing at neighboring ranches. If Bilko was a human "teenager," no doubt he would be declared incorrigible in any court of law. The outfit's wranglers, a somewhat cynical bunch, all want to send Bilko on an expense-paid tour of France—in a can.

© JOHN BARDWELL

Bilko can best be described as a black/brown/sorrel/bay/ dapple-gray. (Never argue politics, religion *or* the color of a horse.) Along with his many talents, Bilko has excellent ears and can hear the door of the grain bin opening from several miles away. He can expertly evaluate a dude's riding ability (or lack thereof) before a foot is even in the stirrup.

Like most fifteen-year-olds, he will invariably try to get away with...well, whatever he can as he takes the path of least resistance. Every month or so one of the wranglers, disgusted with his adolescent antics, will ride him for the day to "tune him up." Bilko always seems to ascertain that this is a prelude to a vacation in Europe and performs like a champion in a national reining competition.

"You know," the wrangler will say afterwards, "this is a pretty good ol' horse. Maybe we should keep him." And he is a pretty good horse—at least for that particular day. Bilko, the consummate fraudster, has once again flimflammed his way out of becoming French cuisine. It works each and every time.

This particular dude outfit entertains guests from strange and exotic places all over the globe. Japan. Great Britain. Israel. Brooklyn. One day, a young couple checks in from the People's Republic of San Francisco. The young woman does not ride and spends her time sketching ranch scenes and skipping after butterflies in the horse pasture. Since their last name contains every letter in the alphabet (sometimes twice), the wranglers, not especially known for their originality, nickname them the Alphabet Couple. Walking by their cabin at night it smells like someone inside is burning skunk weed.

The male half of this couple is a huge, big-bellied guy who wears a little golf hat and a patch over one eye. The wranglers immediately christen him The Polish Pirate—not to his face of course. There is some spirited discussion of this moniker

The Dude Wrangler

Bill Jones gathers black, bay, dunn and other dude horses for yet another ride.

know how things are done in San Francisco, but here in Wyoming we have laws against such weirdness.

One day, I lead a trail ride with Bilko and the Polish Pirate. Bilko, as usual, is lagging about eight thousand yards behind. If he had been walking any slower he would be going backwards. I ride back to check out the problem. Bilko has just stopped for a leisurely little grass snack along the side of the trail. His passenger seems blissfully unconcerned.

"Mr. Lipschitz," I say (names have been changed to protect the lamebrained), "you are going to have to get after Bilko a little bit. I am afraid he will go to sleep while walking, fall and hurt someone. Namely you." I then draw back with an attention-getting little leather quirt I sometimes carry to smack Bilko on the butt.

"You will not abuse this animal in my presence!"

This is a forceful and direct order from the Polish Pirate. I abruptly cancel the quirt activity. Bilko gives me a smug and insolent look.

I think I see him smiling.—*BJ*

because some maintain a real Polish pirate wears a patch over both eyes. Since dudes (how can I say this politically correctly?) who are "weight challenged" are assigned appropriate load-bearing mounts, the Polish Pirate's horse for the week is...Bilko.

On that first morning, while helping saddle the string, I notice the Polish Pirate whispering in Bilko's ear. Bilko eyes him warily as both ears twitch back and forth like two independent metronomes. The Polish Pirate explains he is just trying to determine Bilko's "life force." I patiently explain that I don't

Hallelujah!
Rybecca Panchuk, of Havre, Montana, and Brandi Johnson, of Scottsbluff, Nebraska,
celebrate the sunset and dance in the middle of a dusty western road near Havre.
© Todd Klassy

"Well, the fun's over, but thank God and Greyhound you can always come back!"

"Those cowboys made me laugh!"
© *Larry Angier*

112